NEW ORLEANS

PAUL GREENBERG

Penguin
Random
House

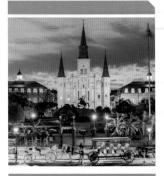

Top 10 New Orleans Highlights

The Top 10 of Everything

CONTENTS

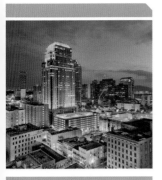

New Orleans Area by Area

Streetsmart

Within each Top 10 list in this book, no hierarchy of quality or popularity is implied. All 10 are, in the editor's opinion, of roughly equal merit.

Throughout this book, floors are referred to in accordance with American usage; i.e., the "first floor" is at ground level.

Front cover and spine *Wrought-iron filigree balconies in the French Quarter*
Back cover *A Mississippi Riverfront streetcar at the Toulouse Street stop in the French Quarter*
Title page *An ornate Mardi Gras mask*

Welcome to
New Orleans

The Crescent City. Birthplace of jazz and home to delicious Creole, Cajun, and Southern food. Wrought-iron railings, lively Mardi Gras, and rumbling streetcars. Voodoo and atmospheric cemeteries. Street musicians and parades. New Orleans is a small city with a huge reputation. With Eyewitness Top 10 New Orleans, it's yours to explore.

Once the wealthiest city in America, thanks to its location at the mouth of the mighty **Mississippi River**, New Orleans has a rich history. Here, French and Spanish influences blend with the Cajun and Creole flavors of Africa and the Caribbean. With its iron filigree balconies and centuries-old houses, the historic **French Quarter** is a living movie set, while the leafier environs of the **Garden District** house postcard-perfect Southern mansions. Stroll along the river or ride the streetcars for evocative tours of the neighborhoods.

New Orleans' passion for the good life is obvious everywhere you walk, from its fine-dining restaurants to the street musicians' jazz soundtrack. Traffic often stops for **daily parades**, which mark everything from weddings to funerals, and the exuberant **Mardi Gras** celebrations, the mother of all free parties, take over the city for a month every year.

Whether you're visiting for a weekend or a week, our Top 10 guide will show you the best of New Orleans: beautiful green spaces such as **City Park** and infamous city hangouts including **Bourbon Street**; **jazz clubs**, where you can see the best local musicians; and testaments to history such as the **National World War II Museum**. There are useful tips and seven easy-to-follow itineraries designed to make the most of the city in a short space of time. Add inspiring photography and detailed maps, and you've got the essential pocket-sized travel companion. **Enjoy the book and enjoy New Orleans.**

Clockwise from top: **French Quarter buildings; the modern skyline; St Mary's Assumption Church; jazz performers in the French Quarter; Botanical Garden; a Mardi Gras costume**

Exploring New Orleans

New Orleans is one of America's most interesting cities, with historic neighborhoods dating back 300 years. There's a lot to take in, so here are some ideas for a two- and four-day city adventure. The real beauty is that you can enjoy the best New Orleans has to offer by just walking around.

The Mississippi Riverfront, with its steamboats, is a great starting point for exploring the city.

Two Days in New Orleans

Day ❶

MORNING

Start with a walk past the steamboats and riverside lawns on the **Mississippi Riverfront** *(see pp22–3)*, then head to the **Audubon Aquarium of the Americas** *(see pp20–21)*, where you can get up close to otters and penguins.

AFTERNOON

After walking and shopping along **Canal Street** *(see pp36–7)*, take the streetcar uptown. Along the way, you can enjoy an inexpensive tour of the Garden District before getting off and heading over to the **Audubon Zoo** *(see pp18–19)*. Spend the rest of the day exploring the sprawling green space of **Audubon Park** *(see p73)*.

Day ❷

MORNING

You can take your time admiring the diverse exhibits in the **New Orleans Museum of Art** *(see pp12–15)*, and visiting the adjoining Sculpture Garden. Stop at the Morning Call Coffee Stand before embarking on a walking or biking tour of **New Orleans City Park** *(see pp16–17)*.

AFTERNOON

Head downtown and buy some local art at **Jackson Square** *(see pp26–7)*, before browsing the galleries and antiques stores of **Royal Street** *(see pp28–31)*. When you've finished, **Bourbon Street** *(see pp32–3)* should be starting to get lively.

Four Days in New Orleans

Day ❶

MORNING

Start your day downtown, with the sights around **Jackson Square** *(see pp26–7)* and the **Mississippi Riverfront** *(see pp22–3)*, including the historic **French Market** *(see p90)*.

AFTERNOON

You can meander toward **Canal Street** *(see pp36–7)* via the antiques shops and art collections on **Royal Street** *(see pp28–31)* before making your way back down **Bourbon Street** *(see pp32–3)*, skipping the seedier bars for world-class jazz clubs.

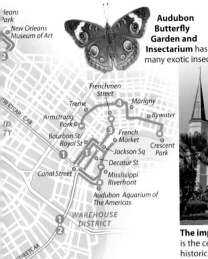

Audubon Butterfly Garden and Insectarium has many exotic insects.

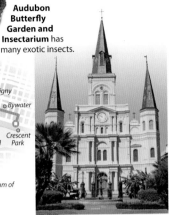

The imposing St. Louis Cathedral is the centerpiece of New Orleans' historic park, Jackson Square.

Key

━ Two-day itinerary
━ Four-day itinerary

Audubon Zoo's entrance features an impressive elephant fountain.

Day ❷

MORNING

Make it a day appreciating the wildlife of New Orleans. Start by spending time uptown at **Audubon Zoo** (see pp18–19). Later, stroll around **Audubon Park** (see p73).

AFTERNOON

Work your way back downtown and head straight to the **Audubon Aquarium of the Americas** (see pp20–21) – combination tickets also allow entry to the **Audubon Butterfly Garden and Insectarium** (see p81).

Day ❸

MORNING

Rent a bicycle and ride around the landscaped greenery of **New Orleans City Park** (see pp16–17), stopping only to wander around the **New Orleans Museum of Art** (see pp12–15).

AFTERNOON

Stroll along **Decatur Street** (see p90), stopping off for food and drinks, before jazz club-hopping your way up **Frenchmen Street** (see p96).

Day ❹

MORNING

Explore **Armstrong Park** (see p97), before stopping for lunch in Treme.

AFTERNOON

Sunset brings out the colors of the houses in the Marigny and Bywater areas, and there's time to see the city skyline from **Crescent Park** (see p98) before dinner.

Top 10 New Orleans Highlights

St. Louis Cathedral, the centerpiece
of New Orleans' Jackson Square

TOP 10 New Orleans Highlights

New Orleans winds gracefully in a crescent shape around a bend in the Mississippi River. The city has a rich French and Spanish cultural history, evident in its food, architecture, and customs. Famous for its carefree vibe, New Orleans is also known for its jazz heritage, colorful festivities, and unmatched *joie de vivre*.

New Orleans Museum of Art

Founded in 1911 by Isaac Delgado, a sugar broker, the New Orleans Museum of Art has a collection of more than 40,000 artworks in 46 galleries, valued at more than $200 million *(see pp12–15)*.

② New Orleans City Park

This park is New Orleans' version of Central Park in New York. A lush, landscaped space with dozens of attractions, it is a popular getaway from the urban bustle *(see pp16–17)*.

Audubon Zoo ③

This world-class zoo has sheltered animals in their natural habitats since 1884 *(see pp18–19)*.

④ Audubon Aquarium of the Americas

One of the finest in the country, this state-of-the-art aquarium houses 15,000 sea animals and features marine life displays *(see pp20–21)*.

⑤ Mississippi Riverfront

New Orleans is bordered by the Mississippi. Take a streetcar ride alongside it, dine by the river, or board a steamboat for a cruise *(see pp22–3)*.

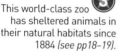

Jackson Square 6

Set in the center of the French Quarter, against the backdrop of St. Louis Cathedral, the attractive Jackson Square is surrounded by beautiful architecture *(see pp26–7)*.

7 Royal Street

One of the most beautiful streets in New Orleans, Royal Street offers the city's best fine art galleries, as well as antiques shops and great restaurants *(see pp28–31)*.

8 Bourbon Street

Bourbon Street features some of the French Quarter's main attractions, including beautiful hotels, excellent vintage restaurants and bars, and plenty of live jazz. This street is a must-see for visitors *(see pp32–3)*.

Mardi Gras 9

Billed as the world's largest street party, Mardi Gras is an annual spring celebration that culminates on Fat Tuesday (just before Lent). This festival, associated with feasting and parties, marks the last celebration before Lent *(see pp34–5)*.

10 Canal Street

Ride the streetcar, enjoy an outdoor lunch, shop at fine boutiques, or try your luck at Harrah's New Orleans Casino on one of the widest boulevards in the world *(see pp36–7)*.

TOP 10 ⭐ New Orleans Museum of Art

The city's oldest fine arts institution, and a historic landmark, the New Orleans Museum of Art, or NOMA, is one of the most important centers of fine arts in the Gulf South. This popular art repository displays works from the Renaissance to the modern era and is the centerpiece of New Orleans' elegant City Park. Its permanent collections and rotating exhibits rival the best museums in the country. NOMA is also a cultural center, hosting high-profile lectures, educational programs, films, and festivals.

① Arts Quarterly
Four times a year, NOMA publishes and distributes this acclaimed full-color magazine. The publication provides updates on new acquisitions and upcoming exhibitions, and informs readers about new trends and historically significant works of art.

② Friday Nights at NOMA
Every Friday at 5pm, NOMA hosts different kinds of special events **(above)**. These include visiting exhibitions, lectures, film screenings, hands-on art workshops, family-friendly activities, and live performances.

③ NOMA Photography Collection
The museum boasts over 14,000 images featuring some of the greatest achievements within the medium. The great photography displayed here includes works by Diane Arbus, Ansel Adams, Man Ray, and Clarence John Laughlin.

④ Museum Shop
No trip to NOMA is complete without a visit to the Museum Shop. It stocks products such as glass art, prints, books, and jewelry, among other things. It also features a local artist every month.

⑤ The Annual Odyssey Ball
The premier event on the city's social calendar, the Annual Odyssey Ball takes place in November. On this day, the museum is beautifully decorated and features auctions, an orchestra, and dancing.

⑥ Modern Art
This display covers the major movements in 20th-century European and American art. The pieces by Andy Warhol are highlights. There are contemporary works too.

THE BUILDING
Most visitors to NOMA are as dazzled by the building as they are by the exhibits inside. The Neo-Classical architecture of the original structure dates back to 1910. It was a gift from sugar broker Isaac Delgado, who envisioned a "temple of art for the rich and poor alike." Wings added in the 1990s complement the original structure, while seamlessly integrating into the surrounding natural environment.

⑦ Café NOMA

The museum café **(left)** is a sleek, atmospheric venue with floor-to-ceiling windows offering views over City Park. It was opened by New Orleans restaurant legend Ralph Brennan. The menu features a range of dishes prepared with fresh, seasonal ingredients supplied by local farmers.

NEED TO KNOW

MAP H2 ■ 1 Collins Diboll Circle, New Orleans City Park ■ 504-488-2631 ■ www.noma.org

Open 10am–6pm Tue–Thu (to 9pm Fri), 11am–5pm Sat & Sun ■ Adm $12 ($10 for seniors and students, $8 for children)

Sydney & Walda Besthoff Sculpture Garden: 10am–6pm Mon–Fri (to 5pm Sat & Sun)

■ Take the Canal streetcar to City Park's main entrance, and walk down the grand promenade to NOMA.

■ Just outside NOMA, Morning Call Café serves *café au lait* (French coffee) and beignets (pastries with powdered sugar).

Facade of NOMA

⑨ Special Exhibitions

In the past, NOMA showcased traveling exhibitions ranging from multimedia works by local and international artists to the Treasures of Ancient Egypt.

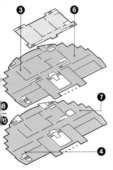

NOMA
Key to Floorplan
First floor
Second floor
Third floor

⑧ Sydney and Walda Besthoff Sculpture Garden

This beautifully landscaped garden features an outdoor collection of more than 60 sculptures **(right)**, most of which were donated by the Besthoff Foundation. Among the works featured here are sculptures by Henry Moore, George Segal, and Barbara Hepworth.

⑩ Wellness Classes in the Sculpture Garden

The Sculpture Garden is a great setting for the yoga classes that take place here every Saturday.

Further Features of NOMA

An Italian Renaissance altarpiece in the European Art collection

1 European Art
French, Italian, Dutch, Flemish, and Impressionist works are showcased in the European Art section. The highlight is a wealth of Italian paintings from the Renaissance to the 18th century. The French collection includes a series of landscape paintings.

2 Louisiana Art
The galleries and period rooms along the mezzanine offer works of art created from the early 19th century in Louisiana. Works by internationally renowned sculptors such as John Scott and Lin Emery can be found in the courtyard and Sculpture Garden.

3 Public Programs
Every Friday the museum remains open until 9pm for special tours, performances, live music, screenings, and interactive workshops.

Artifact from Art of the Americas

4 African Art
This collection is considered one of the most important of its kind in American art museums. It features figures, sculptures, ancient terracottas, textiles, furniture, masks, costumes, marionettes, and musical instruments.

5 Asian Art
NOMA began its collection of Asian art in 1914 with a selection of Chinese jade and stone carvings. Today there are Chinese ceramics, Japanese Edo-period (1603–1868) paintings, and Indian art.

6 Oceanic Art
Tribal art from Polynesia, Indonesia, and Melanesia is at the forefront of this collection from the Oceania region. Do not miss rare pieces from Borneo and the Nias Islands, as well as the fine cotton ritual weavings from Sumatra.

7 Art of the Americas
North, Central, and South American art are the focus here, with works spanning Latin America, Mexico, and the United States. Works displayed range from Mayan artifacts to pre-Columbian artworks, right through to the Spanish-Colonial period. The section also includes a Native American collection dating from ancient times to the present day.

8 Decorative Art
More than 15,000 works comprise this distinctive collection, which covers glass art, American

art pottery, French ceramics, miniature portraits, and furniture. Also on display is a beautiful representation of the works of Fabergé, which includes 44 miniature Easter eggs.

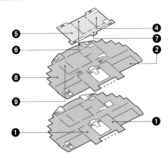

⑨ Photography, Prints, and Drawings

These rotating collections, totaling over 20,000 objects including prints, books, and unique works on paper, are displayed in a special suite of galleries. This particular department has two exhibitions a year. Highlights include works by French artist Henri Matisse.

⑩ Mobile Guides

Free mobile guide tours of the Sydney and Walda Besthoff Sculpture Garden (see p104) are very popular.

PERMANENT EXHIBITS

NOMA's permanent collection includes over 40,000 artworks from all over the world. Among the highlights are rare pieces from the Americas, Asia, and Europe. The collection continues to grow with new acquisitions. Art aficionados will probably notice the preponderance of French and American art.

This portrait of Marie Antoinette was painted by Élisabeth Louise Vigée Le Brun, circa 1788

TOP 10 HIGHLIGHTS

1 Élisabeth Louise Vigée Le Brun's portrait of Marie Antoinette, Queen of France

2 William-Adolphe Bouguereau's painting *Whisperings of Love*

3 Alfred Boisseu's *Louisiana Indians Walking Along a Bayou*

4 Edgar Degas' portrait of Estelle Musson Degas

5 J. S. Copley's *Portrait of Colonel George Watson*

6 An 18th-century Polynesian temple figure, collected by James Cook on his third voyage to the Hawaiian Islands in 1779

7 *Death Comes to the Banquet Table* by Giovanni Martinelli

8 Chinese jade and hard-stone carvings donated by the Morgan-Whitney family

9 *Portrait of Mrs. Asher B. Wertheimer* by John Singer Sargent

10 A vast glass collection, from Ancient Egypt to contemporary creations

TOP 10 ⭐ New Orleans City Park

Built on the site of the former Allard Plantation beside Bayou St. John, New Orleans City Park is one of the biggest urban parks in the country, covering an area of 1,300 acres (526 ha). A perfect spot for children and adults alike, it offers sports facilities, museums, waterways, golf courses, an amusement park, a miniature golf course, a botanical garden, and much more. The park is also home to the New Orleans Museum of Art and the Sydney and Walda Besthoff Sculpture Garden, which showcases over 60 modern sculptures.

New Orleans Botanical Garden ①

Botanical exhibits and themed gardens – including the famous rose gardens – cover 10 acres (4 ha) of this park **(right)**. Sculptures by artist Enrique Alférez stand among the trees.

② Old Oak Grove

New Orleans is home to the world's largest grove of mature oaks **(below)**. The oldest tree here is believed to be over 800 years old.

③ New Orleans Museum of Art

The museum is a big draw in City Park, with magnificent permanent collections and rotating, visiting exhibitions, as well as an adjacent outdoor sculpture garden (see pp12–15).

NEED TO KNOW

MAP H1 ■ 504-482-4888 ■ Canal Street streetcar ■ www.neworleanscity park.com

New Orleans Botanical Garden: open 10am–5pm daily (last adm 4pm); adm $6 for adults, $3 for children

Carousel Gardens Amusement Park: 1 Palm Drive; open 11am–6pm Sat & Sun; adm $4

Train Garden: trains run 10am–4:30pm Sat & Sun; adm $6 for adults, $3 for children

Storyland: 504-483-9402; open 10am–5pm daily (last adm 4:30pm); adm $4

■ The park may seem overwhelming to first-time visitors. You can download a map of the park from the website. Seasonal times and prices vary; check the website for more details.

■ The Morning Call Café is a good place for French desserts and coffee.

Carousel Gardens Amusement Park 4

Featuring one of the last 100 antique carousels in the country, this is a charming amusement park. It also includes a dozen other rides, which make the place a children's wonderland **(right)**.

NOLA CITY BARK

Dog lovers visit City Park all the time, so the park officials created an entire section just for canines called "NOLA City Bark," entered from Magnolia Drive. It has separate facilities for large and small dogs, and those who bring their animals here must subscribe to the annual membership. The park is dotted with shaded areas and flowering trees, and even has a dog wash for messy animals.

Storyland 7

This fairytale playground, with more than 20 exhibits from storybooks, is a major attraction for families. It is an ideal setting for children's parties.

Celebration in the Oaks 8

The park is adorned with decorations and state-of-the-art lighting from Thanksgiving to New Year's Day. This is a favorite stop on most walking tours.

New Orleans City Park

Pavilion of the Two Sisters 5

The semicircular pavilion is built in the style of a traditional European orangery and has become a very popular venue for receptions and fundraisers, as well as other social events.

City Park/ Pepsi Tennis Center 9

With 16 hard and 10 clay courts, this facility offers the best public tennis courts in the state of Louisiana. Visitors can rent equipment, but it is best to book in advance.

City Park Golf Courses 10

A putter's heaven, City Park has two 18-hole golf courses. A championship-level course opened in 2017, featuring historic oak trees and lagoons characteristic of the park.

Train Garden 6

A unique attraction tucked away in the vibrant Botanical Garden is a working miniature-train garden **(right)**, elevated to eye level. It features authentic re-creations of the architectural structures and historic neighborhoods of New Orleans.

⭐ Audubon Zoo

Run by the Audubon Nature Institute, which also maintains the Aquarium of the Americas and the Butterfly Garden and Insectarium, this world-class facility can trace its history back to the 19th century. Today, it is regarded among the finest zoos in the country. Audubon Zoo shelters some of the world's rarest animals and includes interactive exhibits such as Louisiana Swamp, and some entertaining rides, all amid century-old oaks and lush landscaping.

1 Tiger

Audubon Zoo is home to a very rare species of tiger – a magnificent yellow Malayan called Bumi **(above)**. There are only several hundred Malayan tigers left in the wild.

2 Louisiana Swamp Exhibit

The next best thing to a real Louisiana swamp, this exhibit **(below)** features alligators, raccoons, bears, a Cajun houseboat, and Pelicans' Nest, which educates about life in the wetlands and is sponsored by the basketball team of the same name.

3 Kamba Kourse

This exciting four-story adventure ropes course is for visitors of all ages and abilities. Located opposite the giraffes in the African Savanna, it stands even taller than the lofty creatures, with a zenith of 44 feet (13.5 metres).

A RICH HISTORY

Audubon Zoo has existed in various forms for over a century. Originally, animals were exhibited on this site as part of the 1884 World Cotton Exposition *(see p40)*. Many of the zoo's current structures were built by the Works Progress Administration after the Depression in the 1930s. It fell into disrepair in the 1970s and was rebuilt again. Today, this is one of the most well-designed zoos in the country.

4 Asia

Hills, trees, and structures for climbing mean that the Asian elephants and endlessly engaging Sumatran orangutans **(left)** are completely at home in this habitat.

Audubon Zoo

10 Jaguar Jungle

This innovative exhibit highlights the ancient Mayan civilization. The display has recreated ruins along with a simulated archaeological dig site in a tropical rainforest setting. It houses jaguars and spider monkeys, among others.

5 African Savanna

This section of the zoo is home to the large, endangered Southern white rhinoceros **(above)**. Visitors can also see zebras, giraffes, and ostriches here.

6 Red River Hog Habitat

This exhibit comprises two tiny African pigs, Matthew and Isabel, who moved to New Orleans from the Denver Zoo.

7 Reptile House

Here you can get an up-close look at magnificent 200-lb (90-kg) Komodo Dragons and more than 100 species of reptiles.

8 Monkey Hill

Children enjoy climbing this man-made hill, the highest point in the city. At the top are such attractions as a treehouse, tunnel slide, and wading pools.

9 Sea Lions

Among the most entertaining animals in the zoo, the sea lions **(below)** have a special routine for guests. Interestingly enough, their habitat is a popular New Orleans wedding location.

NEED TO KNOW

MAP A6 ■ 6500 Magazine St ■ 504-581-4629 ■ www.audubon natureinstitute.org

Open 10am–5pm Mon–Fri (to 6pm Sat & Sun), closed Mon Sep–Mar ■ Adm $22.95 for adults, $17.95 for children under 13, $19.95 for seniors

■ The trip to the zoo can be as much fun as the destination itself. Catch a streetcar at any point along the historic St. Charles Avenue and see the sights as you make your way to the zoo. The ride takes about 30 mins.

■ Stop at the Zoofari Café, housed in a historic building from the 1930s, to enjoy a burger, hot dog, or chicken wings.

TOP 10 ⭐ Audubon Aquarium of the Americas

An impressive attraction offering visitors the chance to see a white alligator, sharks, seahorses, and a stunning rainforest under one roof, this is one of the premier tourist destinations in the city. Showcasing nearly 500 species of aquatic life, the aquarium is among the most impressive in the country. Massive generator failure after Hurricane Katrina resulted in major losses, but the aquarium triumphantly reopened in 2006 with new sections.

2 Stingray Touchpool

On the second floor of the aquarium, the Stingray Touchpool **(left)** offers visitors a chance to see, and even touch, cownose stingrays. The pool is a favorite with all ages, and visitors get to feed the stingrays.

3 Geaux Fish!

This fun exhibit showcases Louisiana's fishing industry. Hop on a boat, cast a virtual reel, identify local species, or visit a seafood market.

4 Sea Otter Gallery

This habitat **(below)** houses two Southern Sea otters. They live, eat, and play in two huge pools, with rocks and waterfalls. There is also a behind-the-scenes experience for up-close-and-personal visits.

1 Backstage Penguin Pass

Have an intimate, behind-the-scenes encounter with an endangered African penguin in a private enclosure. Learn about how the aquarium cares for its penguins, and visit the Prep Kitchen where their food is prepared. A member of the aquarium's husbandry team guides visitors through and answers any questions.

PARAKEET POINTE

Located on the second floor of the aquarium is Parakeet Pointe, which is an 800-sq-ft (74-sq-m) outdoor environment that is home to hundreds of colorful parakeets. This delightful avian habitat offers visitors an enjoyable interactive experience where they can purchase some seed sticks for a small sum and feed the exotic birds as they stroll through the popular free-flight exhibit.

5 Mississippi River Gallery

This gallery offers a ringside view of the Mississippi's inhabitants. One of the most compelling sights here is Chompitoulas, a blue-eyed white alligator **(above)**. Look out for the catfish, sunfish, and gar.

6 Great Maya Reef

This 4,200-sq-ft (390-sq-m) state-of-the-art reef **(above)** is the opening exhibit of the aquarium. It recreates a submerged city of the Yucatan peninsula. Sea life darts around Mayan stone work and artifacts.

7 Amazon Rainforest

Exotic orchids grow in this superb re-creation of the Amazon rainforest. Piranhas lurk in the flowing waters below the thick forest canopy, inhabited by colorful tropical birds.

8 Penguin Gallery

See these delightful birds **(left)** during the daily feedings (10:30am and 3pm). Don't be surprised by the lack of snow, as the black-footed penguins are from the southwest coast of Africa.

9 Living in Water Gallery

This gallery focuses on the adaptations and behavior patterns that are required by creatures to survive in the water. Colorful clownfish, royal blue tangs, and lionfish can be seen here, as well as anemones and corals.

10 Seahorse Gallery

This section acquaints people with varied and wonderful species of seahorses, many of which are endangered. The aquarium's Project Seahorse is working toward the conservation of the species.

NEED TO KNOW

MAP N5 ▪ 1 Canal Street ▪ 504-581-4629 ▪ www.audubon natureinstitute.org

Open 10am–5pm Mon–Sun; closed Mon Sep–Mar (times vary; check website for latest details) ▪ Adm $29.95 for adults; $21.95 for children under 12; $24.95 for seniors (includes Entergy Giant Screen Theater)

▪ A trip to the aquarium, along with a stroll through the nearby Outlet Collection at Riverwalk along the Mississippi River, can be a day-long excursion. Take a journey down the river on a quaint paddlewheel steamboat.

▪ The aquarium's food court offers basic fast food. No food or drinks are allowed to be brought in from outside. Within walking distance are a few cafés that provide refreshments.

🔟 ⭐ Mississippi Riverfront

Since the 1990s there has been a stunning redevelopment of the Mississippi Riverfront. Businesses, attractions, and special events make this area a must-see for any visitor to New Orleans. A streetcar line runs the length of the riverfront, with stops at all of the popular sites. The riverfront is within walking distance of the Warehouse District, the CBD, and many of the best hotels and restaurants. The long pedestrian path along the riverfront is called the Moonwalk, and is perfect for a romantic stroll.

1 Woldenberg Riverfront Park

This waterfront space **(above)** is one of the most pleasant spots in the downtown area. The park hosts events, concerts, and festivals throughout the year.

2 The Outlet Collection at Riverwalk

This vast indoor complex is two blocks long and faces the Mississippi River. Shop at a variety of retailers and enjoy some of the very best local delicacies that are on offer here.

3 Ernest N. Morial Convention Center

This is the largest convention-center space on a single level in the entire country. It hosts some of the biggest and most prestigious conventions in the world. The center also features state-of-the-art technology.

4 Creole Queen

The best way to experience the Mississippi River is on a two-hour dinner cruise on the Creole Queen **(left)**, an authentic paddlewheel steamboat.

GETTING AROUND THE RIVERFRONT

The riverfront is a vital part of the downtown area. Just across from the JAX Brewery, there is a ticketing kiosk where visitors can purchase tickets for river cruises (some including dinner). Transportation in and around the riverfront is frequent and convenient. The streetcar stops near the Aquarium and runs until 10:30pm daily, while the ferry from downtown to the West Bank of New Orleans runs until just after midnight.

For a key to restaurant price ranges see p77

JAX Brewery **5**

Once a working brewery, today the riverside JAX building **(right)** houses shops, boutiques, and restaurants. A museum traces the history of the brewery.

Entergy Giant Screen Theater **7**

Equipped with an outstanding sound system, the Giant Screen Theater offers a superb viewing experience.

Moonwalk **8**

Running the full length of the riverfront, the Moonwalk is a heavily traveled walkway. Along this stretch there are benches where visitors can relax and watch the river.

The Crazy Lobster Bar and Grill **10**

Indulge in a large bucket of steamed seafood, or try a perfectly grilled lobster along with an icy beer. To top off the perfect meal, sit outdoors, right by the river, and enjoy the live jazz.

Spanish Plaza **6**

Located between The Outlet Collection at Riverwalk and the Audubon Aquarium of the Americas *(see pp20–21)*, the Spanish Plaza is the site of year-round special events and concerts.

Riverfront Streetcar **9**

The bright-red Mississippi Riverfront streetcar **(right)** stops intermittently along the riverfront at all the major shopping and tourist attractions.

Mississippi Riverfront

NEED TO KNOW
MAP N5

The Outlet Collection at Riverwalk : 500 Port of New Orleans; 504-522-1555; www.riverwalk neworleans.com

Ernest N. Morial Convention Center: 900 Convention Center Blvd; www.mccno.com

Creole Queen: 1 Poydras St; 504-529-4567; cruises 2–3:30pm Fri–Sat; adm $27 ($13 for under 12s); www.creolequeen.com

JAX Brewery: 600 Decatur St; 504-566-7245;

10am–7pm daily; www. jacksonbrewery.com

Entergy Giant Screen Theater: 1 Canal St; 504-581-4629; adm $9.95 ($6.95 under 12s, $8.95 for seniors); www.audubonnature institute.org

The Crazy Lobster Bar and Grill: Suite 83, The Outlet Collection at Riverwalk; 504-569-3380; $

■ For the best selection of refreshments head over to The Outlet Collection at Riverwalk.

Following pages Steamboat on the Mississippi River

TOP 10 ⭐ Jackson Square

The elegant centerpiece of the French Quarter, Jackson Square is a lively meeting place. Known as the Place d'Armes in the 1700s, it was later renamed for the Battle of New Orleans hero, Andrew Jackson. His statue dominates the square, with the St. Louis Cathedral providing a majestic backdrop. Quaint shops line the edge of the park, and artists, palm readers, and musicians sell their wares and perform here daily.

1 The Presbytère

Dating circa 1791, this building is part of the Louisiana State Museum. It houses a fabulous Mardi Gras exhibit **(above)**, as well as some of the finest ball gowns and costumes from past Mardi Gras celebrations.

JACKSON SQUARE IN THE MOVIES

If Jackson Square looks familiar even on a first visit, it may be because it has been used as a backdrop in several movies. The square was a featured location in *The Curious Case of Benjamin Button* (2008). The New Orleans Office of Film and Video fields frequent requests for filming on the square, with starring roles in TV shows such as *CSI: New Orleans*, *Treme*, and *Memphis Beat*. Fans of Elvis Presley might recognize the backdrop from his movie *King Creole*.

2 St. Louis Cathedral

This is the oldest continuously active Catholic church in the country **(above)**, first built in 1727, and rebuilt twice since then. The dramatic lighting makes even the back of the church look imposing.

3 Street Musicians

New Orleans is best known for its food and music. The grassroots musicians, who make their living playing on the streets, are most at home in the heart of Jackson Square.

4 Andrew Jackson Statue

Commander of the American forces at the Battle of New Orleans and 7th president of the U.S., Andrew Jackson is commemorated with a bronze statue **(left)** in Jackson Square.

5 Place d'Armes Hotel

Conveniently located right on the edge of the square, the Place d'Armes Hotel is a charming place close to most of the attractions of the French Quarter. Restored 18th- and 19th-century buildings surround a courtyard.

Jackson Square

8 Artistic Community

New Orleans artists do not all need a studio. Many of them work and sell their creations in and around Jackson Square **(below)**.

10 Pedestrian Walkway

Jackson Square's perimeter is lined with stores and boutiques. Pedestrians can spend hours strolling among the musicians, jesters, and artists who work here.

6 Pontalba Apartment Buildings

The oldest apartments in the country (built in the mid-1800s) are among some of the city's most enviable addresses.

9 Faulkner House Books

This two-story building was once home to author William Faulkner. Today, it is a National Historic Landmark and houses a fine bookstore.

7 The Cabildo

The site of the 1803 Louisiana Purchase (see p40) and one of the Louisiana State Museum's buildings, the Cabildo **(below)** features artifacts, artworks, and rotating exhibits highlighting local history.

NEED TO KNOW

MAP M5

The Presbytère and the Cabildo: Jackson Square; 504-568-6968; open 9am–5pm Tue–Sun; adm $6

St. Louis Cathedral: 615 Pere Antoine Alley; 504-525-9585; tours: 1–4pm Wed–Sat; www.stlouis cathedral.org

Place d'Armes Hotel: 625 St. Ann St; 504-524-4531; www.placedarmes.com; $$ (for price categories see p116)

Pontalba Apartment Buildings: St. Peter and St. Ann sts

Faulkner House Books: 624 Pirate's Alley; 504-524-2940; www. faulknerhousebooks.com

■ Enjoy a romantic evening on a mule-drawn buggy around Jackson Square.

■ Try the famous coffee and beignets at the Café du Monde (see p60).

TOP 10 ★ Royal Street

One of the oldest streets in the city, picturesque Royal Street boasts some of the country's best antiques stores and art galleries. Antiques collectors travel here from all over the world to shop at European-style boutiques and visit glass artists and purveyors of fine collectibles. Visitors can stay at historic hotels, enjoy leisurely breakfasts at sunny cafés, or indulge in gourmet cuisine at the numerous specialty restaurants.

1 Cornstalk Hotel

Aptly named because of the cornstalk design on the iron fence around the building, this fine hotel with antique furnishings has old-world charm *(see p116)*.

2 Fleur de Paris

The only boutique of its kind in the South, this lovely shop boasts couture clothing as well as stunning hats for women, all designed and created at the store itself.

3 Court of Two Sisters

This historic restaurant **(below)** was originally a shop owned by two Creole sisters. Today, it is owned by two brothers, but it still retains its original name and is famous for its daily buffet accompanied by live Dixieland jazz.

4 Gallier House Museum

Designed by James Gallier Jr., this grand 19th-century mansion is an amalgam of Creole and American styles. It also inspired local author Anne Rice *(see p41)* to create Louis and Lestat's home in her book *Interview with the Vampire*.

Royal Street

5 Mr. B's Bistro

Located at the corner of Royal and Iberville streets, this restaurant's chief draw is its Creole cuisine. Mr. B's signature dish is the "Gumbo Ya-Ya" (gumbo with pork sausage and chicken).

NEED TO KNOW

MAP L4

Cornstalk Hotel: 915 Royal St; 504-523-1515; www.cornstalkhotel.com

Fleur de Paris: 523 Royal St; 504-525-1899

Court of Two Sisters: 613 Royal St; 504-522-7261; $$$

Gallier House Museum: 1132 Royal St; 504-525-5661; call for timings; adm $15 for adults, $12 for children and seniors; www.hgghh.org

Mr. B's Bistro: 201 Royal St; 504-523-2078; $$$

Hotel Monteleone: 214 Royal St; 504-523-3341

Café Amelie: 912 Royal St; 504-412-8965; $$$

The Supreme Court of Louisiana: 400 Royal St; 504-310-2300

Omni Royal Orleans: 621 St Louis St; 504-529-5333

Rodrigue Studio: 730 Royal St; 504-581-4244; 10am–6pm Mon–Sat; noon–5pm Sun

■ Do not miss the array of interesting boutiques tucked away on the little side streets in the area.

Picturesque building on Royal Street

The Supreme Court of Louisiana ⑧

A massive face-lift has restored this huge stone and marble structure **(right)** to its former glory. The Beaux Arts-style building dates back to 1910 and represents the city's architectural heritage.

⑥ Hotel Monteleone

Founded in 1886, this grand family-run hotel is a New Orleans landmark. A favorite haunt of 20th-century writers, it is still popular with current literati, including Anne Rice and John Grisham *(see p116)*.

⑨ Omni Royal Orleans

Considered one of the area's premier properties, this hotel was built on the site of the 1836 St. Louis Hotel. It has a rooftop pool, and houses the Rib Room, one of the city's finest restaurants *(see p117)*.

⑦ Café Amelie

Enjoy superb Louisiana fare – including shrimp and grits – at this lovely café where diners can bask in the sun. The Princess of Monaco courtyard is 150 years old *(see p60)*.

⑩ Rodrigue Studio

The world-renowned "Blue Dog" paintings **(left)** were created here by Louisiana artist George Rodrigue. Today, his typically Southern art is highly valued.

UPSCALE DINING ON ROYAL STREET

It is only fitting that some of the best fine-dining spots in the city are on this magnificent French Quarter street. A good day on Royal Street would include breakfast at Café Amelie, lunch at the Rib Room, and dinner at Mr. B's Bistro. In between, plan a leisurely cocktail hour at the stylish bar at Omni Royal Orleans Hotel.

For a key to restaurant price ranges see p77

Shopping for Antiques

Walking sticks at The Brass Monkey

1 The Brass Monkey

This store has the largest collection of Limoges boxes in town. The inventory also includes antique walking sticks, Venetian glass, and medical instruments *(see p93)*.

2 Royal Antiques

Boasting some of the most elegant pieces in the French Quarter, this store's collection includes lovely French mirrors, Biedermeier furniture, and Chippendale chairs *(see p93)*.

3 Waldhorn & Adler

MAP M4 ▪ 343 Royal St
▪ 504-581-6379
▪ Closed Sun–Mon

Waldhorn & Adler, housed in a restored building built in 1800 by Edgar Degas' great-grandfather, specializes in 18th- and 19th-century furniture and antique and estate jewelry.

4 Moss Antiques

This store specializes in silver, period jewelry, chandeliers, antique furnishings, and Limoges enamel. The selection of art and sculpture is also noteworthy *(see p93)*.

5 Harris Antiques

MAP M3 ▪ 233 Royal St
▪ 504-523-1605

Harris has one of the largest selections of 18th-, 19th-, and early 20th-century French, Italian, and English furniture, grandfather clocks, and French mantle clocks, as well as antique bronzes and marble sculptures.

6 Keil's Antiques

MAP M4 ▪ 325 Royal St
▪ 504-522-4552

This three-story shop offers thousands of French and English antiques, including chandeliers, jewelry, furniture, and tabletop items. The proprietors of Keil's also own Moss Antiques and Royal Antiques on the same street. The best thing about this store is that there is something for every budget.

7 M.S. Rau Antiques

MAP M4 ▪ 630 Royal St
▪ 504-523-5660

This store has been around since 1912. It is stocked with beautiful jewelry, 18th- and 19th- century fine art, and *objets d'art*. M.S. Rau is also famous for its impressive range of American and European antique furniture.

Gramophone at M.S. Rau Antiques

8 Ida Manheim Antiques

MAP M4 ▪ 409 Royal St
▪ 504-620-4114

Originally a small cabinet shop, today this family-owned store has a fine selection of English, Continental, and Oriental furnishings, porcelains, jade, silver, and paintings.

(9) James H. Cohen & Sons, Inc.

MAP M4 ■ 437 Royal St
■ 504-522-3305

This is the only shop in New Orleans that specializes in rare coins, antique firearms, swords, and unusual collectibles such as old ballot boxes and World War I telescopes.

(10) French Antique Shop

MAP M3 ■ 225 Royal St
■ 504-524-9861

This family-owned store offers a great collection of antique chandeliers and lamps, plus fine art, furniture, and tapestries. Located in the second block of Royal Street, this is the perfect place to begin shopping.

ART SHOPPING ON ROYAL STREET

The art scene in New Orleans is a vibrant and integral part of the city's culture and economy. Galleries flourish in virtually every nook of the city, showcasing works by artists ranging from fresh local talent to renowned names. Exciting new trends and styles have developed out of the city's eclectic culture, and New Orleans is considered to be a key hub of art in the U.S. Serious collectors travel across the world to catch the latest showings. On the first Saturday night of each month, galleries throughout the city hold a wine and cheese open house, where they welcome all visitors to view their latest collections.

Fischer-Gambino is one of the best places in New Orleans for antique furniture and lamps

TOP 10
UNIQUE GALLERIES ON ROYAL STREET

1 Rodrigue Studio (Home of the "Blue Dog")

2 Robert Guthrie Gallery

3 Casell Gallery

4 Angela King Gallery

5 Graphite Gallery

6 Fischer-Gambino

7 Gallery Rinard

8 Elliott Gallery

9 Fredrick Guess Studio

10 Martin Lawrence Gallery

TOP 10 ★ Bourbon Street

This iconic French Quarter street never sleeps. It dates back to 1718, when it was known as Rue Bourbon, and still retains some of the original 18th-century architecture, which can be seen on a leisurely walk down the street. With around-the-clock live music, parties, and all-night bars and clubs, Bourbon Street has an atmosphere of revelry that is unmatched in the city. Renowned restaurants lie interspersed between unique shops and vendors. A night out on Bourbon Street is a once-in-a-lifetime experience.

1 Pat O'Brien's

The infamous "Hurricane" cocktail was invented here in the 1940s. Today, this bar **(below)** offers a lively ambience.

2 Famous Door

This raucous club is packed every night. The Famous Door is a typical all-night Bourbon Street nightclub.

3 Gay and Lesbian Entertainment

Many Bourbon Street restaurants and bars cater to the city's gay and lesbian community. Anchoring the district is the lively Bourbon Pub.

4 Cat's Meow Karaoke Club

With one of the most in-demand stages in the French Quarter, Cat's Meow has pulsating karaoke music, which permeates right through the whole block.

Neon-lit clubs and bars on Bourbon Street

NEED TO KNOW

MAP M3

Pat O'Brien's Bar: 718 St. Peter St; 504-525-4823

Famous Door: 339 Bourbon St; 504-598-4334

Bourbon Pub: 801 Bourbon St; 504-529-2107

Cat's Meow Karaoke Club: 701 Bourbon St; 504-523-2788; www.cats karaoke.com

Royal Sonesta Hotel: 300 Bourbon St; 504-586-0300; www.royalsonesta.com

Chris Owens Club: 500 Bourbon St; 504-523-6400

Preservation Hall: 726 St. Peter St; 504-522-2841

Bourbon House Restaurant: 144 Bourbon St; 504-522-0111; $$$

Lafitte's Blacksmith Shop Bar: 941 Bourbon St; 504-593-9761

Galatoire's Restaurant: 209 Bourbon St; 504-525-2021; closed Mon; $$$

■ It is legal to carry alcohol on Bourbon Street. All the bars have "to go" cups.

For a key to restaurant price ranges see p77

Bourbon Street

7 Preservation Hall

New Orleans jazz echoes through this legendary music hall **(above)**. Veteran jazz musicians and new acts still play here every week.

8 Bourbon House Restaurant

Old New Orleans charm blends seamlessly with a contemporary vibe in this Creole eatery, in the first block of Bourbon Street. Ask for the special Bourbon House Restaurant frozen-bourbon milk punch.

LIVING ON BOURBON STREET

Although known for its unique nightlife, Bourbon Street is also home for many New Orleanians. Many of the facades of the street-facing houses are actually the backs of the homes, built to face lush interior courtyards. Every October, the Historic Bourbon Street Foundation sponsors a "Treasures of Bourbon Street" tour, featuring centuries-old Creole townhouses, cottages, and period architecture.

5 Royal Sonesta Hotel

The Royal Sonesta is on a busy corner of Bourbon Street. Enjoy oysters at The Desire Bar, and see live performances at The Jazz Playhouse (see p117).

6 Chris Owens Club

The eternally youthful entertainer Chris Owens takes to the stage six nights a week at her club. For decades now, she has been providing her patrons with a Las Vegas-style variety show that never seems dated.

9 Lafitte's Blacksmith Shop Bar

This late-18th-century Creole cottage **(below)** may look decrepit, but it houses one of the French Quarter's nicest watering holes. This is one of the best spots for people-watching in the area.

10 Galatoire's Restaurant

A wonderful place to dine in the city, Galatoire's has an old-world charm and fabulous cuisine. The soufflé potatoes are a must-try.

🔟 ⭐ Mardi Gras

New Orleans bills its annual Mardi Gras celebration as "the biggest street party in the world." More than a million visitors gather in the city up to three weeks before the festival. Lavish parades are staged by various clubs, or "krewes," along with street gatherings and parties. New Orleans is the place to be during this time to let your hair down, don an outrageous costume, vie for beads thrown from parade floats, and generally party hard for the last time before Lent.

① Bourbon Street Awards Costume Contest

This LGBT costume contest, held on Mardi Gras afternoon, showcases some of the most outrageous and imaginative costumes of the festival. Staged on Bourbon Street, it attracts thousands of locals and visitors alike.

④ Krewe of Rex Parade

The crown jewel of New Orleans' Mardi Gras is the Krewe of Rex Parade **(right)**. Rex has reigned as King of the Carnival since he first appeared in 1872, and he has since defined the festival with the royal colors of purple, green, and gold.

② Krewe of Zulu Parade

Just before the Rex Parade is the Krewe of Zulu **(above)** on the morning of Mardi Gras. The Zulu Social Aid and Pleasure Club produces one of the most festive parades, inspired by one of the fiercest tribes in all of Africa.

③ Krewe of Endymion Parade

Considered one of the longest and most elaborate parades, Endymion rolls out on the Saturday before Mardi Gras. The Endymion ball is one of the most popular in town and continues all night.

⑤ Krewe of Armenius Gay Mardi Gras Ball

The gay community produces some of the most elaborate Mardi Gras balls. The Krewe of Armenius throws camp and uproariously funny balls. Their costumes are among the best in the city.

BLAINE KERN'S MARDI GRAS WORLD

Blaine Kern is the master Mardi Gras float designer and builder in New Orleans, and his Mardi Gras World is a year-round facility open to the public. Here, visitors can see how the props and floats are conceived, designed, and constructed. Giant character heads and extravagant floats from past Mardi Gras festivals are displayed in this building. The space is also rented out for private parties and receptions (see p48).

Krewe of Bacchus 6

The Bacchus Parade **(right)** on the Sunday before Mardi Gras features more than 25 floats, including some of the largest and longest, such as the King Kong, the Queen Kong, and the heralded Bachagator.

Mardi Gras Parades on St. Charles Avenue 10

On Mardi Gras, groups of friends and families stake out their territory along the historic St. Charles Avenue to watch the Rex and Zulu parades, as well as the "everyman" truck parades that follow them.

Krewe du Vieux 7

If it can be mocked, the Krewe du Vieux will do so in their highly anticipated parade. Typical themes of this popular group tend to be satirical and bawdy.

Krewe of Muses 8

Named for the daughters of Zeus in ancient Greek mythology, Muses is one of the few all-female krewes. They delight crowds by throwing lavishly decorated shoes on their parade route from Magazine and Jefferson.

Krewe of Barkus Dog Parade 9

Every year, dog owners dress themselves and their pets in matching costumes and parade through the French Quarter **(left)**. Dog parade themes include "A Street-Bark Named Desire" as well as "Tail House Rock."

NEED TO KNOW

■ Mardi Gras is celebrated on the Tuesday before Lent, but celebrations begin as early as January 6, with the night of the Epiphany (the festival marking the revelation of God as Jesus Christ).

■ The crowd is usually well behaved, but be careful with your personal items. Stay on streets that are highly populated. Be warned that a lot of alcohol is consumed during Mardi Gras, so try to steer clear of drunken revelers.

■ Bars are open citywide during Mardi Gras, although not necessarily for food. Either bring your own or try the snacks available from street vendors. On St. Charles Avenue, people generally bring their own coolers and snacks with them.

TOP 10 ⭐ Canal Street

One of the broadest streets in America, the 170-ft (52-m) wide Canal Street runs across New Orleans, from the Mississippi to Lake Pontchartrain. The main activity is around the CBD, where luxury hotels, upscale restaurants, and fine retail establishments line both sides of the street. The Canal streetcar line runs down the middle of the thoroughfare, providing access to Mid-City and the theaters.

2 Shops at Canal Place

Right by the Mississippi, this complex of offices, stores, restaurants, and theaters **(left)** is dominated by the upscale Saks Fifth Avenue.

3 Theaters on Canal Street

Two prominent theaters face each other across Canal Street – the 1940s Art Deco Joy Theater and the 1927 Saenger Theatre with an Italian-style courtyard. Sensitive renovation has seen both restored to their past glory.

Streetcars on Canal Stree

4 Palace Café

Housed in an elegant early-20th-century building, the three-story Palace Café serves contemporary and delicious Creole cuisine. Do not miss the crabmeat cheesecake and the white chocolate bread pudding *(see p85)*.

6 Harrah's New Orleans Casino

This casino is the only land-based one in the city (the other two are on boats). The property includes table games, slot machines, fine restaurants, a luxurious hotel, and an ice bar.

CANAL STREETCAR

To take in the city's sights at a leisurely pace, the Canal streetcar is a great option. This is the best way to see the architecture and layout of the city, all the way from the Mississippi to the historic cemeteries in the Mid-City area, while the Rampart-St. Claude line serves the bohemian Faubourg Marigny and Bywater neighborhoods. Tickets for the streetcar cost just $1.25.

1 The Ritz-Carlton, New Orleans

A historic structure that once housed a department store, this building has been elegantly refashioned into the Ritz-Carlton Hotel. The hotel has 450 guest rooms and is home to a world-class spa, stylish restaurant M Bistro, and nightly live jazz *(see p116)*.

5 Canal Street Ferry Line

Commuters traveling from the East Bank of New Orleans to the West Bank often use the ferry line at the foot of Canal Street. Passengers can also drive their cars onto the ferry **(below)**.

8 The World Trade Center

The imposing 33-story World Trade Center **(left)** soars above the banks of the Mississippi. There are plans to transform the tower, which has been closed since Hurricane Katrina, into a lavish hotel.

10 Rubensteins

The city's oldest house of fine fashion, Rubensteins stands at the corner of Canal Street and St. Charles Avenue. This menswear store has been providing quality fabrics and tailoring since 1924.

7 Audubon Butterfly Garden and Insectarium

Located in the old U.S. Customs House, this museum offers up-close insect encounters, insect cuisine, an animated insect movie, and a chance to "shrink" yourself to insect size.

9 The Roosevelt New Orleans

This grand hotel opened in 1893 as the Grunewald, and is now part of the Waldorf Astoria hotel group. It features the historic Sazerac Bar and the legendary Blue Room, used for weddings and private events *(see p116)*.

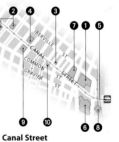

Canal Street

NEED TO KNOW

MAP E4

Shops at Canal Place: 333 Canal St; 504-522-9200

Palace Café: 605 Canal St; 504-523-1661

The Ritz-Carlton, New Orleans: 921 Canal St; 504-524-1331

Harrah's New Orleans Casino: 8 Canal St; 504-533-6000; www.harrahs neworleans.com

Audubon Butterfly Garden and Insectarium: 423 Canal St; 504-524-2847; open daily 10am–5pm; adm $22.95 for adults, $17.95 for children, $19.95 for seniors; www.audubon natureinstitute.org

The World Trade Center: 2 Canal St; 504-529-1601

The Roosevelt New Orleans: 130 Roosevelt Way; 504-648-1200

Rubensteins: 102 St. Charles Ave; 504-581-6666

■ Be sure to cross Canal Street at designated cross walks only.

The Top 10 of Everything

The jazz band at New Orleans' historic Preservation Hall

TOP10 Moments in History

Jean Baptiste Le Moyne de Bienville

1 Founding of New Orleans (1718)

Jean Baptiste Le Moyne de Bienville of the French Mississippi Company founded a colony on the Lower Mississippi and named it "La Nouvelle Orléans." Situated on a curve of the Mississippi River, the site was thought to be immune to hurricanes and floods. Surrounded by the river, lakes and swamps, it also became known as the Île d'Orléans.

2 New Orleans becomes a Spanish Colony (1763)

New Orleans was ceded to the Spanish in 1763 by Louis XV. However, the French settlers rebelled and forced governor Antonio de Ulloa to abdicate. It was General Alexander O'Reilly who established Spanish control in 1768. Thereafter, the Spanish encouraged trade and turned the city into a commercial hub.

3 The Great French Quarter Fire (1788)

Of 1,100 buildings in New Orleans, 856 were destroyed by a fire on Good Friday in 1788. At the time, the city had only two fire vehicles, and both were destroyed. After the fire, the city was rebuilt with Spanish-style colonial architecture.

4 Construction of the St. Louis Cathedral (1794)

Although the original St. Louis Church was destroyed by the fire of 1788, by the following year the cornerstone of the new St. Louis Cathedral was in place. This was the third Roman Catholic church to be built on this site since 1718, but it was the first to be elevated to cathedral status.

5 First Mardi Gras Celebrated (1827)

During Spanish rule, pre-Lent festivals were banned. By 1823, New Orleans had been under U.S. rule for 20 years (the U.S. bought Louisiana from the French through the Louisiana Purchase of 1803), and, around 1827, the people were finally permitted to wear masks and celebrate. The first proper Mardi Gras parade was held 10 years later.

Poster advertising Mardi Gras

6 World Cotton Exposition (1884)

The 1884 World Cotton Exposition lasted six months. Up to a third of all cotton produced in the U.S. was handled in New Orleans, home of the Cotton Exchange. However, despite its scale, this fair was a financial disaster riddled with debt and corruption, especially as treasurer Edward A. Burke absconded with much of its budget.

⑦ New Orleans Saints Football Franchise Awarded (1966)

On All Saints Day in 1966, the National Football League awarded New Orleans the league's 16th major team franchise. The aptly named Saints adopted a gold fleur-de-lis as their team symbol, representing the French colonists who had settled in Louisiana.

The Louisiana Superdome

⑧ Construction of the Louisiana Superdome (1975)

It took four years and $163 million to build the enormous Louisiana (now Mercedes-Benz) Superdome. The result is an architecturally stunning facility *(see p80)*.

⑨ Louisiana World Exposition (1984)

The centerpiece of this event was a gondola lift that ferried millions of visitors across the Mississippi River. The fair was the precursor to a major redevelopment of the city's riverfront area.

⑩ Hurricane Katrina (2005)

The largest natural disaster in the U.S., Hurricane Katrina hit New Orleans on August 29, 2005. The failing of the levees caused massive flooding and destruction, from which the city has now mostly recovered.

TOP 10 NEW ORLEANS FIGURES

1 Marie Laveau (1801–81)
Known as New Orleans' "Voodoo Queen," Laveau practiced the religion that originated in West Africa.

2 Louis Armstrong (1901–71)
Armstrong, also known as "Satchmo," is globally remembered as a premier jazz trumpeter and singer.

3 Mahalia Jackson (1911–72)
Long heralded as the "Queen of Gospel Music," Jackson recorded 35 albums during her career.

4 Tennessee Williams (1911–83)
Playwright Williams captured the angst of the American South in his works, including *The Glass Menagerie*.

5 Truman Capote (1924–84)
During his controversial career, Capote authored some of the best-selling novels of his time, including *In Cold Blood*.

6 Stephen Ambrose (1936–2002)
Historian Stephen Ambrose famously chronicled the presidencies of Richard Nixon and Dwight D. Eisenhower.

7 Anne Rice (b.1941)
America's master scribe of horror novels, Rice is the author of the *Vampire Chronicles* series.

8 Ellen Degeneres (b.1958)
The famous comedienne hosts a well-known talk show, and has appeared on stage and in movies.

9 Emeril Lagasse (b.1959)
Now a TV personality, Lagasse is renowned as a chef, restaurateur, and cookbook author.

10 Harry Connick, Jr. (b.1967)
This award-winning jazz musician is also a talk show host and movie star.

Author Anne Rice

ᴛᴏᴘ10 Museums and Galleries

opened in 2000, the 56th anniversary of the Normandy invasion. It honors the Americans who took part in World War II. The museum also celebrates the New Orleans shipbuilder Andrew Higgins and explores the war's amphibious troop invasions (see p79).

3 Confederate Memorial Hall Museum

MAP Q3 ▪ 929 Camp St ▪ 504-523-4522 ▪ 10am–4pm Tue–Sat ▪ Adm ▪ www.confederatemuseum.com

Veterans of the Civil War have donated most of the memorabilia housed in this museum. Founded in 1891, the Confederate Memorial Hall has a collection of American flags, uniforms, artwork, weaponry, and more than 500 rare photographs including ambrotypes and tintypes.

1 Contemporary Arts Center New Orleans

Housed in a stunning 30,000-sq-ft (2,800-sq-m) building, the Contemporary Arts Center (CAC) honors an eclectic collection of art genres covering music and dance, kinetic sculpture, drawings, and paintings. The CAC also hosts multidisciplinary workshops in the performing arts (see p80).

2 The National World War II Museum

Founded by historian Stephen Ambrose, this large museum

4 New Orleans Museum of Art

Established in 1911, the New Orleans Museum of Art, or NOMA, is the oldest repository for art in the city. Permanent collections include rare French and American pieces, including Claude Lorrain's *Ideal View of Tivoli,* and a stunning Native American collection. Works by the masters, including Picasso, Renoir, Monet, Gauguin, and Pollock, are on display. The museum also includes a sculpture garden (see pp12–15).

The exterior of the National World War II Museum

Louisiana Children's Museum

5 Louisiana Children's Museum

This multilevel facility, moving to New Orleans City Park in late 2018, offers kids a hands-on art and craft experience, with interactive exhibits and activities for the whole family. It has outreach programs that make classroom teaching more vibrant *(see p82)*.

6 Ogden Museum of Southern Art

The huge collection of contemporary art here focuses on artists from the South. It includes pieces by father and son Benny and George Andrews, and works by folk artist Clementine Hunter. There is an after-hours program on Thursdays with live music and special exhibits *(see p80)*.

7 New Orleans African American Museum

MAP K3 ▪ 1418 Governor Nicholls St ▪ 504-566-1136 ▪ 11am–4pm Wed–Sat ▪ Adm ▪ www.noaam.org

Located in Treme, home to the oldest African-American community in the country, this museum is housed in a lovely Creole villa dating from 1828. Rotating exhibits chart the art, history, and culture of African-Americans in New Orleans and the diaspora. Highlights include original African beads, masks, musical instruments, and religious objects from Congo.

8 Southern Food & Beverage Museum

MAP R1 ▪ 1504 Oretha C. Haley Blvd ▪ 504-569-0405 ▪ 11am–5:30pm Wed–Mon ▪ Adm ▪ www.natfab.org

New Orleans locals joke that they are either eating, or talking about their next meal. So it's only fitting that there should be a museum dedicated to the city's vibrant culinary scene. The Southern Food & Beverage Museum (SoFAB) traces the history of food across all cultures, while the Museum of the American Cocktail, located in SoFAB, celebrates local drinks from absinthe to the Sazerac *(see p57)*.

9 Historic New Orleans Collection

Used mainly as a resource by serious researchers, the Historic New Orleans Collection also attracts curious visitors who can learn about the city through its many historical artifacts. Established in 1966, the Historic New Orleans Collection is a repository of manuscripts, artistic exhibits, and documents showcasing the varied cultures that have shaped the city *(see p90)*.

Historic New Orleans Collection

10 New Orleans Jazz Museum at the Old U.S. Mint

MAP L6 ▪ 400 Esplanade Ave ▪ 504-568-6993 ▪ 9:30am–4:30pm Tue–Sun ▪ www.musicatthemint.org

Part of the Louisiana State Museum portfolio, the comprehensive Jazz Museum's displays include a 1917 disc of the first jazz recording.

🔟 Architectural Highlights

The beautiful, elaborately decorated interior of St. Patrick's Church

1 St. Patrick's Church

The subtle Gothic exterior of the church belies its ornate interior. Built in the early 19th century, the original building was overhauled to create a much grander structure with a 185-ft- (56-m-) high bell tower. The altar, windows, and doorways are in Gothic style, while 16 stunning stained-glass windows form a wonderful half dome over the altar (see p82).

2 Lafitte's Blacksmith Shop Bar

The oldest building in the French Quarter was built in 1772 by alleged slave-traders Pierre and Jean Lafitte. Considered to be the longest continually operating bar room in the country, it is still lit by candlelight (see p33).

3 The Supreme Court of Louisiana

The Supreme Court of Louisiana building is an imposing edifice made of stone and marble. The 1910 structure is an example of Beaux-Arts architecture, with its arched windows and Classical pilasters. Once in ruins, this landmark building was restored to its previous glory with a major $50-million renovation (see p29).

4 Hotel Monteleone

The 1886 luxury hotel underwent a $60-million renovation in 2004, but has retained its original grandeur. Grab a cocktail at the revolving Carousel Bar (see p116).

5 Mercedes-Benz Superdome

This stadium is home to the New Orleans Saints football team. The dome covers the world's largest steel-constructed space unobstructed by posts. Considered to be one of the premier sports venues in the country, the stadium has hosted six National Football League Super Bowls (see p80).

Mercedes-Benz Superdome

6 The Cabildo

One of five properties making up the Louisiana State Museum, the Cabildo *(see p27)* was originally built in 1795, destroyed in the fire of 1788, and rebuilt. The Cabildo was the site where the Louisiana Purchase was signed in 1803 *(see p40)*.

7 Napoleon House

Now a restaurant, this early 19th-century landmark was originally the home of New Orleans mayor, Nicholas Girod, who offered it as a refuge for Napoleon during the latter's imprisonment at St. Helena *(see p95)*.

8 Pontalba Apartment Buildings

Built in 1849 by the French Baroness Pontalba, these apartment buildings, the oldest in the U.S., reflect both French and American architecture, with cast-iron galleries and Creole-style floor plans *(see p27)*.

Pontalba Apartment Buildings

9 The Peristyle at City Park

MAP H2 ▪ 1 Palm Drive ▪ 504-482-4888 ▪ www.neworleanscitypark.com
The Neo-Classical Peristyle, built in 1907, is supported by massive Ionic columns and guarded by four stone lions. A stairway leads down to the picturesque Bayou Metairie waterway.

10 St. Louis Cathedral

The triple steeples of this Jackson Square landmark make it one of the city's most striking and recognizable buildings. Inside, visitors can admire stained-glass windows, paintings, and a Rococo-style gilded altar *(see pp26 & 90)*.

TOP 10 PUBLIC ART SITES

Blaine Kern's Mardi Gras World

1 Blaine Kern's Mardi Gras World
Watch carnival floats and figures being made at this warehouse *(see p48)*.

2 Sydney and Walda Besthoff Sculpture Garden
The sculpture garden is an outdoor installation at NOMA *(see pp12–15)*.

3 Enrique Alferez Sculptures
These graceful sculptures are artfully placed throughout the New Orleans City Park *(see pp16–17)*.

4 Train Garden at Botanical Garden
This exhibit features an eye-level New Orleans cityscape and running miniature train *(see p17)*.

5 "Ocean Song" Kinetic Sculpture
MAP N5 ▪ Woldenberg Park
These eight pyramids depict the movement of the Mississippi.

6 Louis Armstrong Statue
The jazz legend is immortalized in this 12-ft- (4-m-) high statue in Armstrong Park *(see p97)*.

7 Poydras Corridor
MAP N1 ▪ Poydras St
This rotating sculpture exhibition has included works by Southern artists of local and international acclaim.

8 Joan of Arc Maid of Orleans Statue
MAP L5 ▪ St. Philip St. at Decatur St.
This golden bronze statue is a replica of a 19th-century sculpture by French sculptor Emmanuel Frémiet.

9 Murals at Sazerac Bar
The Art Deco murals in the Roosevelt hotel bar date to the 1930s *(see p116)*.

10 Auseklis Ozols Murals at Windsor Court Hotel
These remarkable murals depict famous New Orleanians in the Grill Room of the hotel *(see p116)*.

TOP 10 Off the Beaten Path

Touring the Louisiana swamplands

some stunning cemeteries to be found citywide; Metairie Cemetery is particularly well kept.

④ New Orleans Historic Voodoo Museum
MAP L4 ■ **724 Dumaine St** ■ **504-680-0128**
There are a lot of misconceptions about the practice of voodoo, and the New Orleans Historic Voodoo Museum is the best place to learn more about it. As well as exhibits on the history of voodoo and presentations of voodoo art, there is a voodoo priest on site to give readings and answer questions.

New Orleans Historic Voodoo Museum

① Swamp Tours
504-689-4186 ■ **www.jeanlafitteswamptour.com**
It is easy to forget that New Orleans sits right in the middle of a vast expanse of swampland, but take a drive just a short way out and the reality is hard to ignore. Swamp tours offer a great way to view some wildlife. The boats take visitors into the Bayou to see deer, alligators, mink, turtles, and snakes.

② New Orleans Ghost Tour
MAP K4 ■ **718 North Rampart St** ■ **504-666-8300** ■ **www.frenchquarterphantoms.com**
The city's colorful and sometimes gory history means that downtown is as haunted a neighborhood as you'll find anywhere in the country. Three hundred years' worth of ghosts and ghouls inhabit the historic buildings of the French Quarter, and French Quarter Phantoms ghost tours bring the undead to life.

③ Cemetery Tours
Metairie Cemetery ■ **5100 Pontchartrain Blvd** ■ **8am–5pm daily**
In New Orleans, people are usually buried above ground rather than below. This is because the city is technically below sea level, and therefore deep digging is not allowed in some areas. There are

⑤ Second Line Parades
Throughout the year the various historic social clubs and bene-volent associations in New Orleans organize huge Second Line parades led by a brass band (the main/first line). People in festive dress follow the band, singing, dancing, and waving handkerchiefs in the air. Visitors can join in or apply to the City for a permit to form their own line.

6 NOLA Social Ride
877-734-8687 ■ www.nola
socialride.org

Biking around New Orleans is always fun, but it's even better doing it with an enthusiastic bunch of locals who love to share their insider tips and knowledge of the city. This free ride-along takes place every week, with varying routes, a happy, friendly crowd, and the odd bar stop.

7 Pharmacy Museum
MAP M4 ■ 514 Chartres St
■ 504-565-8027 ■ 10am–4pm Tue–Sat
■ Adm ■ www.pharmacymuseum.org

The country's largest museum of pharmaceutical memorabilia, the Pharmacy Museum holds medical instruments, medicine vials, and prescriptions from the Civil War. It also houses voodoo potions and a fascinating exhibit about epidemics of the 19th and 20th centuries.

8 Museum of Death
MAP M3 ■ 227 Dauphine St
■ 504-593-3968 ■ www.museum
ofdeath.net/nola

The city has a unique perspective on death, and even funerals are celebratory affairs with music, dance, and a parade. What better location, then, for this strangely life-affirming museum dedicated to all things deathly, from rituals to serial killers to all manner of morbid artifacts.

Bull riding at the prison rodeo in Angola

9 Prison Rodeos
Louisiana State Penitentiary, 134 miles (216 km) NW of New Orleans ■ 225-655-2607
■ www.angolarodeo.com

Twice a year, in April and October, the Louisiana State Penitentiary holds a full rodeo on its premises in Angola. The convicts participate in bareback riding, wild horse races, bull riding, chariot races, and wild cow milking; some of them also sell their handi-crafts at heavily secured stalls. It is an interesting day out, and tickets always sell out fast.

10 Burlesque
Don't fall for the lurid strip clubs on Bourbon Street – there's a much more tasteful, artistic, and often tongue-in-cheek striptease option, supplied by New Orleans' thriving burlesque scene. Look at the calendars for the AllWays Lounge *(see p51)* and The HiHo Lounge *(see p100)*. SoBou restaurant has a delightfully kitsch "legs and eggs" burlesque brunch *(see p61)*.

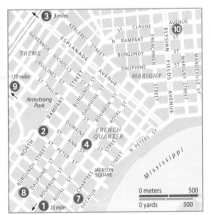

🔟 Children's Attractions

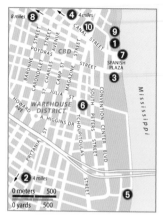

3 Jean Lafitte Swamp Tours

6601 Leo Kerner Lafitte Parkway, Marrero ▪ 504-689-4186 ▪ Call for rates ▪ www.jeanlafitte swamptour.com

New Orleans is surrounded by swamps that are home to varied plants and wildlife. The best way to see this unique ecosystem is from a swamp boat. The tour is an exciting excursion for families.

4 Storyland

Children can enjoy a bit of old-fashioned fun at City Park's theme playground, Storyland, where fairy tales are brought to life. These delightful creations include Captain Hook's pirate ship, Pinocchio's whale, and Jack and Jill's hill. Children can clamber all over the structures (see pp16–17).

1 Entergy Giant Screen Theater

A five-and-a-half-story screen with a spectacular sound system shows 3-D films, providing a larger-than-life viewing experience at the Entergy Giant Screen Theater. Watch features on underwater adventures, historical re-enactments, real footage of natural disasters, and docudramas on nature (see p23).

2 Audubon Zoo

This zoo is home to a rare white tiger, orangutans, elephants, and bears, among others. Ride the Swamp Train, or fly through the trees on Kamba Kourse, an adventure ropes course, which towers above the giraffes. Kids will love the tree-house and the slide on Monkey Hill. Viewing the animals in their simulated natural habitats is an entertaining and educational experience (see pp18–19).

A character at Storyland

5 Blaine Kern's Mardi Gras World

MAP S5 ▪ 1380 Port of New Orleans Place ▪ 504-361-7821 ▪ 9:30am–4:30pm daily ▪ Adm ▪ www.mardi-grasworld.com

This vast warehouse displays Mardi Gras memorabilia, including floats and costumes. Most of the exhibits are created by the artist Blaine Kern.

Zebras at Audubon Zoo

Children playing at the educational Louisiana Children's Museum

6 Louisiana Children's Museum

Although it is an educational venue for children, this museum will also appeal to inquisitive and playful adults. Wonderful interactive displays, such as the Little Port of New Orleans or the Eye to Eye (where you can step inside a giant eyeball), make this a novel way to learn *(see p82)*.

7 Creole Queen

Nothing can give you the true feeling of being in New Orleans as much as a journey down the Mississippi River on a paddlewheel steamboat. During the cruise, you'll enjoy the captain's narration, rich with history and anecdotes, and see the city from the water. Visitors can also enjoy a dinner buffet and jazz music on the special Creole Queen dinner cruise *(see pp22 & 23)*.

8 Shrine on Airline
6000 Airline Dr ▪ 504-734-5155 ▪ Timings vary by event ▪ Adm ▪ www.milb.com

Also known as Zephyr Field, this stadium has 10,000 seats and seating for another 1,000 people on the nearby levee overlooking center field. The $21-million facility built after Hurricane Katrina has added amenities such as a swimming pool, luxury suites, and two hot tubs. The stadium is not only for fans of the Baby Cakes baseball team, formerly known as the Zephyrs, but also hosts various kinds of entertainment too.

9 Audubon Aquarium of the Americas

At the edge of the Mississippi River, the aquarium houses approximately 15,000 aquatic creatures and nearly 500 species. Do not miss the Great Maya Reef Tunnel, which allows a view of underwater life usually reserved for divers, and the Seahorse Gallery *(see pp20–21)*.

10 Audubon Butterfly Garden and Insectarium

More than 70 live insect exhibits are on display here. There are also giant animatronic bugs and a gift shop with insect-themed products. Visitors can also sample insect cuisine at the Bug Appetit café or watch butterflies in the Asian garden *(see p37)*.

Butterfly at the Asian garden

Performing Arts Venues

1 BB's Stage Door Canteen

MAP Q3 ■ 945 Magazine St ■ 504-528-1943 ■ www.nationalww2museum.org

Performances at this venue in The National World War II Museum *(see p79)* include big bands, swing dancing, comedy, and jazz nights.

BB's Stage Door Canteen

2 Joy Theater

MAP N4 ■ 1200 Canal St ■ 504-528-9569 ■ www.thejoytheater.com

The Art Deco fixtures, including a glowing marquee, make this theater an evocative venue for films, comedy shows, and other productions.

3 Saenger Theatre

MAP N4 ■ 1111 Canal St ■ 504-525-1052 ■ www.saengernola.com

Over $50 million were spent restoring the Saenger to its former glory, complete with its famous blue sky domed ceilings and twinkling stars.

It plays host to large musical acts, as well as the most popular touring Broadway and musical productions.

4 Lupin Theater, Tulane University

MAP B5 ■ McWilliams Hall, Tulane University ■ 504-865-5105 ■ www.neworleansshakespeare.org

The Shakespeare Festival at Tulane is the only professional theater event in the South dedicated to the works of the Bard. Performances take place here every summer. The Lupin Theater also schedules arts in education programs through the year.

5 Mahalia Jackson Theater of the Performing Arts

This 2,243-seat theater, named for the famous gospel queen, is located on Basin Street. On any given night, the audience can experience top-name artists, the Louisiana Philharmonic Orchestra, Broadway companies, ballet troupes, and other performers *(see p98)*.

6 Contemporary Arts Center New Orleans

Among the many attractions here is an intimate theater that features musical artists, original stage plays, big-band concerts, and emerging performance artists. The venue is often the setting for cutting-edge performances *(see p80)*.

The restored Saenger Theatre

Concert at the Lakefront Arena

7 University of New Orleans Lakefront Arena

6801 Franklin Ave ■ 504-280-7222
■ www.arena.uno.edu

The large Lakefront Arena has hosted everything from big-name music artists and sports events to colorful Disney stage productions. Artists such as Christina Aguilera, Lynyrd Skynyrd, Motley Crue, and Kelly Clarkson have all taken the stage here.

8 Orpheum Theater

MAP M2 ■ 129 Roosevelt Way
■ 504-274-4871 ■ www.orpheum
nola.com

Located in the revived Theater District, the Orpheum is a favorite venue of the Louisiana Philharmonic Orchestra. In addition to music performances, it stages everything from comedy to burlesque.

9 Smoothie King Center

MAP P1 ■ 1501 Dave Dixon
Drive ■ 504-587-3822 ■ www.
smoothiekingcenter.com

This 17,000-seat facility often hosts sporting events. It also doubles as a venue for artists such as Elton John and the Red Hot Chili Peppers.

10 AllWays Lounge and Theatre

MAP K4 ■ 2240 St. Claude Ave
■ 504-218-5778 ■ www.theallways
lounge.net

This comfortable venue, well loved by the city's creative types, puts on a range of shows, including full-scale musicals, stand-up comedy, drag, and burlesque. The building also houses the fringe Theatre at St. Claude.

TOP 10 MOVIES THAT WERE FILMED IN NEW ORLEANS

1 A Streetcar Named Desire (1951)
This film, based on Tennessee Williams' play, has stunning performances by Marlon Brando and Vivien Leigh.

2 Easy Rider (1969)
Counterculture bikers travel from Los Angeles to New Orleans searching for freedom in this iconic film.

3 Pretty Baby (1978)
Twelve-year-old Brooke Shields stars in this controversial picture about Storyville, New Orleans' historic red-light district.

4 Steel Magnolias (1989)
A touching movie about the bond between a group of Southern women.

5 Sex, Lies, and Videotape (1989)
Highly erotic, this movie showed the sultry sensuality of New Orleans.

6 JFK (1991)
This Oliver Stone production dealt with the controversies around the assassination of John F. Kennedy.

7 The Pelican Brief (1993)
New Orleans figured prominently in this riveting thriller about a student who uncovers a conspiracy.

8 Interview With a Vampire (1994)
Anne Rice's tale of the vampire Lestat de Lioncourt starred actors Tom Cruise, Brad Pitt, and Kirsten Dunst.

9 Dead Man Walking (1995)
In this crime drama Susan Sarandon plays a New Orleans nun fighting to abolish the death penalty.

10 Ray (2004)
An Academy Award-winning movie on the life of jazz pianist Ray Charles.

Interview With a Vampire (1994)

TOP 10 Live Music Venues

The stage at well-known New Orleans blues club The Howlin' Wolf

1 The Howlin' Wolf
MAP Q4 ■ 907 South Peters St
■ 504-522-9653

This club, named for bluesman Chester Burnett, or "Howlin' Wolf," is known for attracting big names such as Harry Connick, Jr., Alison Krauss, Foo Fighters, Dr. John, and many more. The unique carved bar is from a hotel once owned by the famed gangster Al Capone.

2 Candlelight Lounge
925 N. Robertson St
■ 504-525-4748

One of the few remaining music clubs in Treme, this modest venue is especially popular for its acclaimed weekly Wednesday night acoustic concerts held by the Treme Brass Band, but the jazz, soul, funk, rap, and R&B is great any night.

A band at Candlelight Lounge

3 Maple Leaf Bar
MAP A4 ■ 8316 Oak St
■ 504-866-9359

The Maple Leaf Bar attracts an eclectic crowd of college students and people in their 30s and 40s. Big names, such as the Rebirth Brass Band, perform here, but it also promotes upcoming musicians.

4 Pat O'Brien's
There are often queues to get in, but the line is as much fun as the ambience inside. The music is lively and the courtyard restaurant is not to be missed (see p32).

5 Siberia
MAP K4 ■ 2227 St. Claude Ave ■ 504-265-8855
■ www.siberianola.com

Expect acts toward the punkier end of the scale at this venue, with electronic dance music and the local "bounce" rap featuring strongly, too. There's also a free weekly comedy show.

6 One Eyed Jacks
MAP L3 ■ 615 Toulouse St
■ 504-569-8361 ■ www.oneeyed jacks.net

Indie rock, electronica, and punk are staples of the calendar here, as are huge dance parties hosted by the city's best-loved DJs. The decor is bordello chic.

7 Maison
MAP K6 ■ 508 Frenchmen St
■ 504-371-5543 ■ www.maison
frenchmen.com

Maison usually has a jazz-oriented line-up, but its three stages allow for a wider variety of acts. The dinner menu and lack of cover charge most nights make it a popular spot, and early arrivals are encouraged.

8 Davenport Lounge
Upscale, laid-back luxury characterizes this lobby-level lounge at the Ritz-Carlton hotel (see p37). Furnished with beautiful 19th-century antiques, the lounge is named for famous jazz trumpetist and singer Jeremy Davenport, who provides the evening's entertainment.

Jazz act at local pub Tipitina's

9 Tipitina's
MAP C6 ■ 501 Napoleon Ave
■ 504-895-8477

This tiny neighborhood pub draws some of the hottest jazz and rock acts in Louisiana and from farther afield.

10 Mid-City Lanes Rock 'n' Bowl
MAP B3 ■ 3000 South Carrollton Ave
■ 504-861-1700

This bowling alley doubles as a music and dance venue. Go bowling, stay on for a show and food, then dance until the wee hours of the morning.

TOP 10 JAZZ CLUBS

A trumpetist at Snug Harbor

1 Snug Harbor
MAP K6 ■ 626 Frenchmen St
■ 504-949-0696
A jazz musician's club, with decent food.

2 Arnaud's
Live Dixieland jazz, plus a selected "jazz" menu at a fixed price (see p95).

3 Palm Court Jazz Café
MAP L5 ■ 1204 Decatur St
■ 504-525-0200
Live traditional jazz and Creole cuisine.

4 Sweet Lorraine's
MAP K4 ■ 1931 St. Claude Ave
■ 504-945-9654
Great atmosphere, a stellar sound system, and the best jazz in town.

5 The Three Muses
MAP K6 ■ 536 Frenchmen St
■ 504-298-8746
Local jazz and a great cocktail menu.

6 Preservation Hall
Dedicated to preserving the classic New Orleans jazz tradition (see p33).

7 Fritzel's European Jazz Pub
MAP L4 ■ 733 Bourbon St
■ 504-586-4800
Since 1969, this intimate jazz hub has attracted the best musicians.

8 The Bombay Club
MAP M3 ■ 830 Conti St
■ 504-586-0972
Classy, with live music every weekend.

9 House of Blues
MAP N4 ■ 225 Decatur St
■ 504-310-4999
World-renowned musicians play here.

10 Maison Bourbon
MAP L4 ■ 641 Bourbon St
■ 504-522-8818
Popular for its diesel-strength mojitos and traditional Southern jazz.

🔟 Gay and Lesbian Venues

1 OZ

One of the city's most popular dance clubs, OZ has a vibrant atmosphere, a superb sound system playing high-energy music, great DJs, and several fun weekly events, including Drag Bingo, or "Dingo," "Boy Next Door" contests, themed performances, and daily happy hours from 4 to 8pm. It is open 24 hours on weekends but Thursday is particularly lively – billed as the "Totally Awesome 80s night," it includes a male strip show at midnight *(see p94)*.

The popular dance club, OZ

2 Big Daddy's
2513 Royal St ▪ 504-948-6288

Situated slightly off the beaten path in the Faubourg Marigny, Big Daddy's is a small neighborhood lounge bar that is open 24 hours a day, and popular with locals. With an intimate atmosphere, great cocktails and a pool table, this venue also has some of the friendliest bartenders in New Orleans. A party atmosphere kicks off late at night.

3 The Country Club
634 Louisa St ▪ 504-945-0742

Housed in an elegant 19th-century Italianate Center Hall mansion in the Bywater neighborhood, The Country Club offers relaxation as well as exciting evening events. Visitors can choose from a number of options, including the restaurant serving Creole South cuisine by executive chef Chris Barbato, a bar, pool, Jacuzzi, spa and massage services, a large movie screen, and cocktails on the veranda. The saltwater pool, hot-tub and sauna set amid lush greenery are the club's highlights.

4 Napoleon's Itch
MAP L4 ▪ 734 Bourbon St
▪ 504-371-5450

Located in Bourbon Street, the center of gay nightlife in New Orleans, Napoleon's Itch is a quiet, upscale bar with a sleek, contemporary interior and an outdoor area – a perfect place to relax. The impressive drinks menu specializes in a large selection of mojitos and martinis. On Friday and Saturday nights it livens up with dance music.

⑤ Bourbon Pub-Parade Disco
MAP L4 ■ 801 Bourbon St ■ 504-529-2107

Regarded as the anchor of the gay and lesbian entertainment district in New Orleans, the Bourbon Pub-Parade Disco is the largest out of the longest continuously operating gay clubs in the U.S. The pub downstairs is constantly packed with patrons watching videos on large screens. Upstairs, the raucous Parade Disco has a dance floor, great DJs, and a variety of live entertainment, including contests, cabarets, and male dancers.

⑥ Good Friends Bar
MAP L4 ■ 740 Dauphine St ■ 504-566-7191

A slightly older crowd frequents the warm and welcoming Good Friends Bar. Tuesday nights are reserved for karaoke. The Queen's Head Pub upstairs has a wrap-around balcony and arranges a piano-bar singalong on Sunday evenings.

Good Friends Bar, an old favorite

⑦ 700 Club
MAP L4 ■ 700 Burgundy St ■ 504-561-1095

This chilled-out neighborhood venue has a fun atmosphere. The bar serves cocktails and craft beer, while the kitchen serves bar food, including burgers and fried catfish, until late. The "everyone welcome" philosophy means there's always a friendly crowd.

⑧ The Phoenix
MAP K6 ■ 941 Elysian Fields Ave ■ 504-945-9264

This is one of the most frequented leather bars for the gay community of New Orleans. The Eagle Bar, upstairs, is a popular meeting spot for locals. This place is packed every Friday and Saturday night.

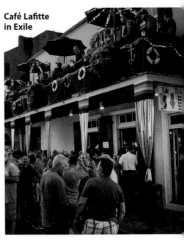

Café Lafitte in Exile

⑨ Café Lafitte in Exile
MAP L4 ■ 901 Bourbon St ■ 504-522-8397

Founded in 1933, this is the oldest gay club in the U.S. and the former haunt of Tennessee Williams and Truman Capote. Today it has two floors of state-of-the-art sound systems and a large video screen. Café Lafitte's balcony is one of the most coveted spots in the city, especially during Mardi Gras. The weekly Wednesday night karaoke and Sunday "Trash Disco" are huge draws.

⑩ The Friendly Bar
MAP K6 ■ 2301 Chartres St ■ 504-943-8929

True to its name, this bar has a congenial ambience and friendly bartenders who always greet guests. The DJ plays great music, and the lively pool table and warm banter make this a great place in which to relax over a beer.

Regional Dishes

1 Alligator Sauce Piquante
Traditionally, Cajuns used spicy sauce piquante in dishes made with rabbit. Alligator sauce piquante is a variation that uses the tail meat of an alligator, combined with heavy seasonings, including cayenne pepper, garlic, green chilies, onions, black pepper, and jalapeno peppers.

2 Court Bouillion
A staple in Louisiana Cajun households, court bouillion is essentially a seafood stew, but there are several variations. The two most popular use redfish or catfish. The recipe always features garlic, onion, and celery. Learning to cook this dish requires a lot of practice.

3 Blackened Redfish
Local chef Paul Prudhomme popularized the culinary method of blackening. The redfish recipe calls for the fish to be rubbed with Cajun spices and then cooked on high heat in a cast-iron skillet. The process can be used for chicken, catfish, and other meats and fish.

Rice-based dish Jambalaya

4 Seafood Gumbo
Gumbo can be safely called the official food of New Orleans (next to red beans and rice, of course). It is a rich, thick dark soup with mixtures of seafood, such as crab, shrimp, catfish, oysters, or whatever the cook desires. Gumbo can also be made using chicken or sausage meat.

Seafood gumbo

5 Jambalaya
Both French and Spanish influences have shaped the jambalaya. This rice-based Creole dish is a bit like paella. Some make it with seafood, while others use chicken, sausages, or both. Tomatoes, celery, and even-handed seasoning are all key to perfecting this dish.

6 Oysters Bienville
Named after the founder of New Orleans, this unique dish was created during the Great Depression at Antoine's, the oldest family-run restaurant in the country. The oysters are topped with béchamel, sherry, cayenne, garlic, shallots, and minced shrimp, and then baked on rock salt with a breadcrumb-and-cheese topping.

7 Fried Green Tomatoes with Shrimp Rémoulade
Green tomatoes have a rich flavor, but in New Orleans the taste is enhanced by frying them in batter and adding fresh Gulf shrimps and tangy rémoulade sauce. A staple dish in the best restaurants of the city.

8 Muffuletta

Legend has it that New Orleans' old Central Grocery was a gathering spot for local workers. Holding bread in one hand and meat in another, they would engage in lively debates, and food would fly. The owner eventually put the meat between slices of bread, added olive salad, and invented the muffuletta.

9 Barbecued Shrimp

Not to be confused with foods cooked in bottled barbecue sauces, these shrimps are smoked and then cooked with Worcestershire sauce and black pepper. The best dishes are made with jumbo Gulf shrimps, which are slow cooked. The secret to making delicious shrimp is to use a generous amount of real butter.

Barbecued shrimp

10 Po' Boys

Sandwiches made of crispy French bread with ingredients such as shrimp, catfish, oysters, beef, ham, crab, and even French fries. Ubiquitous in New Orleans.

A classic Po' Boy sandwich

TOP 10 DRINKS

Mint Julep, a refreshing cocktail

1 Mint Julep
Iconic in the American South, Mint Juleps are a fragrant mix of bourbon, mint, sugar, and water.

2 Sazerac
Dating from the Civil War, this cocktail contains Cognac, rye, herbsaint (or absinthe), and bitters.

3 Ramos Gin Fizz
Also called New Orleans Fizz, a Ramos Gin Fizz includes gin, lemon, lime, egg white, cream, sugar, and orange-flower water, as well as soda water.

4 Hurricane
This powerful sweet rum drink is the signature cocktail at the French Quarter's Pat O'Brien's bar *(see p32)*.

5 Cajun Martini
Simply adding a shot of jalapeno-infused vodka turns an ordinary martini into a hot and spicy sensation.

6 Mimosa
The Sunday brunch drink of choice is a mixture of fresh orange juice and champagne or sparkling wine.

7 Abita Beer
Brewed in nearby Abita Springs, Louisiana, Abita has eight flagship brews and five seasonal brews.

8 Pimm's Cup
This summery New Orleans favorite is a fruity, gin-based cocktail. It was invented in the mid-19th-century in England as a health tonic.

9 Vieux Carré
This potent whiskey cocktail was first concocted in the Carousel Bar of Hotel Monteleone *(see p29)*.

10 Cajun Bloody Mary
Not just any old Bloody Mary will do – people in New Orleans add hot sauce and horseradish to this classic cocktail.

🔟 Restaurants

The serene, leafy surroundings of refined restaurant Commander's Palace

1 Commander's Palace
Known for its impeccable service and gracious ambience, Commander's excels with the house turtle soup, crab cakes, and its signature white chocolate bread pudding. Ask for a table in the Garden Room (see p77).

2 La Petite Grocery
Chef Justin Devillier was named the Best Chef: South at the 2016 James Beard Awards, thanks to stand-out dishes including blue crab beignets and turtle bolognese. The traditional New Orleans cuisine is served in a century-old building that has previously housed a coffee and tea depot, grocery store, butcher shop and florist (see p77).

3 Compère Lapin
Housed in the hip Old No. 77 Hotel, chef Nina Compton's popular eatery has received rave reviews for its unique melting pot of Carribean, French, Italian, and Creole cuisines. The ever-changing menu has diverse dishes such as cold smoked tuna tartare and curried goat with sweet potato gnocchi (see p85).

4 August
This is the flagship restaurant of renowned local chef John Besh. Upscale and elegant, this downtown eatery features creative dishes such as pan-roasted sable fish with truffled potatoes. Besh is known for his use of special seasonings and local ingredients (see p85).

5 Arnaud's
This restaurant has served the city since 1918. Featuring both classic and innovative Creole dishes, the menu is matched by the elegant ambience and exemplary service. Shrimp Arnaud, oysters Bienville, and speckled trout meunière are among the specialties here (see p95).

Seafood at Arnaud's

6 Atchafalaya
Brunch is served from Thursday to Monday at this intimate uptown spot. Its Bloody Mary bar and mouthwatering Creole menu attracts locals looking for Louisiana specialties, such as boudin cake. Dinner is a romantic affair, with dimly lit dining rooms on two levels and a creative menu that doesn't feel pretentious (see p77).

7 Dooky Chase

During her long career, Leah Chase has won every culinary award possible, and she still plays a part in ensuring that her fried chicken is world-class. Even former President Obama dined here. Locals navigate the unusual opening hours to sit down with a plate of heaven *(see p107)*.

8 Mr. B's Bistro

Anchoring the corner of Royal and Bienville streets in the French Quarter, this casually elegant bistro prepares dishes such as Gumbo Ya-Ya (made with chicken and spicy sausage) and a honey-ginger glazed pork chop. Sunday brunch is a treat: try the barbecued shrimp *(see p29)*.

9 Brigtsen's

Frank Brigtsen worked in some of New Orleans's finest kitchens before opening his own award-winning Creole restaurant in a quaint uptown house. Enjoy hearty comfort food dishes such as roasted duck and sesame-crusted rabbit with spinach *(see p77)*.

10 Shaya

Chef Alon Shaya serves up high-end Israeli food. The rush to reserve a table was already in full swing by the time the restaurant won Best New Restaurant in the U.S. in 2016. Head over for lunch, when crowds are less intense *(see p77)*.

High-end dining at Shaya

TOP 10 PLACES FOR LATE-NIGHT DINING

The interior of Clover Grill

1 Clover Grill
MAP L4 ▪ 900 Bourbon St ▪ 504-598-1010 ▪ $
Burgers and breakfast dishes are always on the menu at this 24-hour eatery.

2 Trolley Stop Café
MAP S1 ▪ 1923 St. Charles Ave ▪ 504-523-0090 ▪ $$
The ideal place for gooey egg dishes, waffles, pancakes, and burgers.

3 Port of Call
Great burgers and cocktails *(see p101)*.

4 13 Monaghan
MAP K6 ▪ 517 Frenchmen St ▪ 504-942-1345 ▪ $
This laid-back bar serves huge po'boys.

5 Camellia Grill
MAP A4 ▪ 626 S. Carrollton Ave ▪ 504-309-2679 ▪ $
Sit at the counter for fried apple pie, cheeseburgers, and crispy French fries.

6 Angeli
MAP L5 ▪ 1141 Decatur St ▪ 504-566-0077 ▪ $$
The spot for salads, pizzas, and pasta.

7 Ernst Café
MAP P4 ▪ 600 South Peters St ▪ 504-525-8544 ▪ $$
Sophsticated bar food includes crawfish stew and gumbo.

8 Turtle Bay
MAP L5 ▪ 1119 Decatur St ▪ 504-586-0563 ▪ $$
Enjoy pizza, burgers, and icy Abita beer.

9 St. Charles Tavern
MAP R2 ▪ 1433 St. Charles Ave ▪ 504-523-9823 ▪ $$
Roast beef po'boys, biscuits topped with sausage, and pizza are on the menu.

10 Siberia
Tasty Slavic soul food is on offer at this popular nightclub *(see p101)*.

For a key to restaurant price ranges see p77

Cafés

1 Feelings Café
MAP F3 ■ 2600 Chartres St
■ 504-945-2222

This intimate restaurant is tucked away in a residential area. The lively piano bar and elegant courtyard would be reason enough to visit, but the real draw is the chef's seafood stuffed eggplant with shrimp, crawfish, and sausage.

2 Vic's Kangaroo Café
MAP P4 ■ 636 Tchoupitoulas St
■ 504-524-4329

Known for its beers on tap, Vic's is usually loud and crowded. It also has some great Australian specialties on the menu.

3 Café du Monde
MAP L5 ■ 800 Decatur St
■ 504-525-4544

Since 1862, locals have relied on Café du Monde for their morning coffee with chicory and beignets (fried pastries with powdered sugar), a New Orleans specialty. The café has multiple locations, but the anchor restaurant is the one in the city's French Quarter.

Café du Monde

Plaque at the Bon Ton Café

4 Bon Ton Café
MAP P3 ■ 401 Magazine St
■ 504-524-3386

The Bon Ton has been in business since the early 1900s. Local specialties such as turtle soup, gumbo, and crabmeat au gratin share menu space with a respectable selection of steaks and chops. The bread pudding with whiskey sauce is a must.

5 Café Amelie
MAP L5 ■ 912 Royal St
■ 504-412-8965

Sunday brunch at Café Amelie is served in its beautiful courtyard. The menu is limited but expertly executed, and the ambience is second to none. Highlights include crab cakes with a citrus drizzle.

6 Café Rose Nicaud
MAP K6 ■ 632 Frenchmen St
■ 504-949-3300

This laid-back spot is a good alternative to the busier Marigny cafés, especially if you're up later than you'd planned. It has excellent coffee and a breakfast menu that includes alligator sausage with biscuits, along with vegan, vegetarian, and gluten-free options.

Diners enjoying a meal at Café Degas

 Café Degas

For a true French café experience, head to Café Degas. The restaurant offers everything from a light hors d'oeuvres menu and a stellar Salade Niçoise, to a perfect Dijon-crusted rack of lamb *(see p107)*.

8 Cake Café & Bakery
MAP F3 ▪ 2440 Chartres Ave
▪ 504-943-0010

This cute independent bakery serves locally sourced, innovative dishes. Try the gooey-centered chocolate-almond croissants, fresh bagels and, during Mardi Gras, fabulous King Cakes.

9 La Madeleine Bakery Café
MAP A4 ▪ 601 S. Carrollton Ave
▪ 504-861-8662

It is hard to know which is more irresistible here – the elegantly presented pastry selection or the hearty home-made soups. La Madeleine, ostensibly a bakery, turns out some outstanding hot entrées, pastas, and chicken dishes. It also offers one of the best cups of coffee in town.

10 Who Dat Coffee Café
MAP F3 ▪ 2401 Burgundy St
▪ 504-872-0360

This small but lively coffee shop, located in the Marigny neighborhood, serves delicious coffee. Don't miss out on the tasty jalapeno corn bread.

TOP 10 BREAKFAST SPOTS

1 Dante's Kitchen
MAP A4 ▪ 736 Dante St
▪ 504-861-3121
The Mississippi blueberry pancakes served here are a must-try.

2 Satsuma
3218 Dauphine St ▪ 504-304-5962
A hip, friendly local diner serving healthy breakfast options.

3 SoBou
MAP M4 ▪ 310 Chartres St
▪ 504-552-4095
Enjoy legs with your eggs at this slick eatery's fun burlesque brunch.

4 Café Adelaide
Try Café Adelaide's honeycomb waffles with toasted pecan syrup *(see p85)*.

5 Brennan's
Bananas Foster and Eggs Sardou have been on the menu since 1946 *(see p95)*.

6 Eat
MAP L4 ▪ 900 Dumaine St
▪ 504-522-7222
From the grillades to the fresh bagels, breakfast here is hearty and filling.

7 Slim Goodies Diner
MAP G6 ▪ 3322 Magazine St
▪ 504-891-3447
This place offers hearty eggs, meat, and potatoes breakfasts. Cash only.

8 Camellia Grill
The omelets here are made fresh and grilled in front of guests *(see p59)*.

9 Ruby Slipper
MAP M3 ▪ 2001 Burgundy Street
▪ 504-525-9355
The Marigny branch of a popular diner.

10 Mother's
MAP P4 ▪ 401 Poydras St
▪ 504-523-9656
Enjoy eggs cooked any style and fresh biscuits with meat to start the day.

A prawn dish at Mother's

TOP 10 Shops and Markets

Entrance to Shops at Canal Place

4 Rubensteins
Since 1924, Rubenstein Brothers has been one of the most respected purveyors of menswear in New Orleans. Detailed tailoring and personal attention define the service here [see p37].

5 Fifi Mahony's
In New Orleans, you could easily need a last-minute wig for a spontaneous costume party, and this funky French Quarter boutique is just the place. Experienced staff take you through the fitting [see p93].

1 Shops at Canal Place
This multipurpose center on the edge of the French Quarter offers theaters, cafés, restaurants, and upscale retailers. Shoppers can easily spend a whole day browsing stores such as the multilevel Saks Fifth Avenue, Pottery Barn, Ann Taylor, Coach, and Brooks Brothers, among others [see p36].

2 Mignon Faget
Original jewelry items designed by Mignon Faget are on sale in this store. Her elegant and sometimes quirky designs are inspired by the natural surroundings and man-made structures of New Orleans. The store also stocks beautiful home-decor pieces, including glassware, linens, and baby gifts [see p76].

3 Adler's Jewelry
Around since 1898, Adler's has been the top jeweler in New Orleans for over a century. The firm is still owned by the family that founded it, and buyers from around the world come here to find unique pieces. They have an extensive giftware line, as well as a range of locally inspired items, including New Orleans-themed holiday ornaments and Mardi Gras jewelry [see p84].

6 Trashy Diva
MAP S3 ▪ 2048 Magazine St ▪ 504-299-8777

This boutique specializes in colorful fitted dresses with eye-catching patterns. There's a wide selection of garments, from special-occasion cocktail dresses to everyday wear with a vintage flavor. Next door, its sister stores sell equally fabulous lingerie and shoes.

Dress from Trashy Diva

7 Fleur de Paris
Housed in a historic building, Fleur de Paris is known internationally for its custom millinery and couture gowns. European-trained milliners create exquisite one-of-a-kind hats on site, with antique flowers, feathers, veiling, and silk ribbons [see p29].

Renowned milliner Fleur de Paris

⑧ Krewe de Optic

MAP L5 ▪ 809 Royal St

▪ 504-684-2939

A tropical climate with year-round sunshine demands stylish sunglasses, and this boutique has an exciting range of styles inspired by the city's diverse cultures. The frames are made from high-quality plastics, and everything from the hinges to the lenses is engineered with care, making for highly desirable pieces.

Browsing at the French Market

⑨ The French Market

Sitting at the edge of the Mississippi River, the picturesque French Market is a conglomeration of an outdoor farmers' market, a covered flea market, shops, arts and crafts boutiques, and restaurants. The lively market is also the site of a number of special events, jazz concerts, and festivals that take place throughout the year (see p90).

⑩ The Outlet Collection at Riverwalk

Locally owned businesses and national retailers blend nicely in this large waterfront complex. The mall, built on the site of the 1984 Louisiana World Exposition (see p41), offers tax-free shopping for international visitors looking for small souvenirs, clothing, home-decor items, and even the latest high-tech games. There are also several restaurants, bars, and fast food joints (see p23).

TOP 10 SOUVENIRS AND KEEPSAKES

Traditional ceramic masks

1 Ceramic Masks
The tradition of Mardi Gras masking is enshrined in locally made ceramic masks. A wonderful holiday keepsake.

2 Mardi Gras Beads
Although they are usually made of plastic, the colorful Mardi Gras beads that are caught from float-riders are considered as precious as gold.

3 Voodoo Dolls
These exquisitely detailed figures are sold at stores all over the city. They are authentic, colorful representations of the local voodoo tradition.

4 Bourbon Street T-Shirts
There are souvenir t-shirt shops on most blocks in the French Quarter.

5 New Orleans Coffee Beans
The best local coffees are made by Community Coffee and Luzianne and are sold all over the city.

6 Jambalaya Mix
A great way to take home a taste of New Orleans is with the Cajun food producer Zatarain's jambalaya mix.

7 Red Beans and Rice Mix
Delicious and easy to make, red beans and rice make up the official "Monday night dish" in New Orleans.

8 Cajun Spices
Chefs such as Emeril Lagasse and others take pride in their secret spice mixtures, available for sale citywide.

9 Pat O'Brien's Hurricane Glass
Pat O'Brien's bar mixes powerful "Hurricane" drinks. Guests even get to keep the glass (see p32).

10 Restaurant Cookbooks
The best chefs in town have their own cookbooks, which are usually for sale in their restaurants.

New Orleans for Free

1 Food on Game Day

Every Sunday, fans of the New Orleans Saints football team gather in bars to follow the team's ups and downs. Most bars serve up plates of local delicacies for free.

2 Stand-up Comedy

The comedy scene in New Orleans is always growing, and visitors can see stand-up shows featuring local and touring comedians for free every night of the week. The best are at The Howlin' Wolf *(see p52)* on Tuesday nights and the AllWays Lounge *(see p51)* on Saturday nights.

3 Commemorate History

Chalmette Battlefield; Jean Lafitte National Historical Park; 8606 West St. Bernard Highway, Chalmette; 504-281-0510; www.nps.gov/jela ■ Navy Week: www.nolanavyweek.com

New Orleans' turbulent history is commemorated in many ways, and its various battles to retain its identity are remembered. The anniversary of the Battle of New Orleans, in January, sees a huge reenactment at Chalmette Battlefield. During Navy Week, in April, historic tall ships line the shores of the Mississippi along the Warehouse District, the French Quarter, and the Marigny.

4 Mardi Gras

■ Across the city ■ www.mardigrasneworleans.com

The largest free party on the planet sees a month or so of parades and parties all over the city, culminating on the big day itself. Look at the schedule and see which parades take your fancy – there's everything from miniature floats to dogs in costume.

Masked reveler at Mardi Gras

5 Mini Music Festivals

Summers are long in New Orleans, but the city rewards those who brave the heat with a choice of mini music festivals that last just one evening. The various series run at Armstrong Park *(see p97)*, Lafayette Square *(see p82)*, and Algiers Point on the West Bank, and involve many big local names.

6 Museums for Free

St. Mary's Assumption Church: MAP J5; 923 Josephine St; 504-522-6748 ■ Germaine Wells Mardi Gras Museum: MAP M3; Arnaud's, 813 Bienville St (enter via restaurant); 504-523-5433; www.arnaudsrestaurant.com/about/mardi-gras-museum

The city of New Orleans is a living museum in many ways, but visitors can also discover more detailed information about its history. Try the Historic New Orleans Collection *(see p90)*, St. Mary's Assumption Church, and the Germaine Wells Mardi Gras Museum for a look at the diverse aspects of the city.

Tall ships on the Mississippi during Navy Week

(7) Learn to Dance
MAP K4 ▪ 2358 St. Claude Ave
▪ 504-383-5284 ▪ www.nolajitter
bugs.com

New Orleans has a wealth of wonderful music on offer, but, to get into the swing of things, it pays to know how to dance. NOLA Jitterbugs Dance School hosts a choice of free dance lessons at venues around the city. Beginners are always welcome.

(8) Year-Round Festivals
French Quarter Festival:
http://fqfi.org ▪ Bayou Boogaloo:
Bayou St. John, Mid-City;
www.thebayouboogaloo.com

New Orleans celebrates everything from food to music. The best free festivals include the music weekends of the French Quarter Festival and Bayou Boogaloo, as well as the festivities surrounding Halloween and St. Patrick's Day.

Jazz performers on Frenchmen Street

(9) Jazz on Frenchmen Street
MAP K6 ▪ Frenchmen St

There's nothing like an evening bouncing from club to club, dipping into the music that takes your fancy as you pass by each open doorway. Many venues don't charge a cover.

(10) NOLA Brewery Tours
MAP R4 ▪ 3001 Tchoupitoulas St
▪ 504-896-9996 ▪ Tours: 2–3pm Fri, 2–
4pm Sat & Sun ▪ www.nolabrewing.com

Get a glimpse behind the scenes of a local brewery during free tours of the NOLA facility on Friday and Saturday afternoons. The free samples are a popular part of the tour.

Streetcars in New Orleans

TOP 10 BUDGET TIPS

1 Public transport – both buses and streetcars – is very cheap, so it's worth making the most of it.

2 Visitors can buy a good-value Jazzy Pass for cheaper fares, with 1-, 3-, and 30-day passes available.

3 Many restaurants and bars have a happy hour around 4–6pm, often with some very good deals.

4 Look in unusual places for free concerts, from St. Louis Cathedral *(see p90)* to the Old U.S. Mint *(see p92)*.

5 Take the ferry instead of a cruise for a riverside view of the city skyline.

6 Visit during the low season, which runs from June to September.

7 Plan well ahead for Mardi Gras and major festivals such as Jazz Fest. Prices spike as they approach.

8 Go for a walk. Most neighborhoods in the city are compact enough that visitors do not have to use taxis.

9 Take a free tour of the French Quarter, run by Free Tours by Foot. Book online: www.freetoursbyfoot.com

10 In season, many bars host crawfish or shrimp boils, and you can eat for a small set price.

A heaped plate of crawfish

🔟 Festivals and Events

Visitors at the popular New Orleans Wine & Food Experience

1 New Orleans Wine & Food Experience

504-529-9463 ■ www.nowfe.com

During the NOWFE, held every May, local restaurants host vintner dinners, while daytime hours are spent in seminars, and at cooking demos. The Grand Tasting is a huge event at the Mercedes-Benz Superdome (see p80).

2 Mardi Gras

New Orleans is internationally known for its Carnival celebrations that gear up about three weeks before Lent. Mardi Gras itself draws a million tourists each year for street parties, parades, and masked balls. The more risqué side of Carnival happens in the French Quarter, while family celebrations happen in neighborhoods all over town (see pp34–5).

3 French Quarter Festival

504-522-5730 ■ www.fqfi.org

Every April, for one weekend, the French Quarter turns into a 15-square-block street party. Stages are set up all over the Quarter and top jazz, rock, hip-hop, and Cajun bands play to huge audiences. In Jackson Square and the nearby Woldenberg Park local restaurants serve their signature drinks and dishes from makeshift booths.

4 Go Fourth on the River

www.go4thontheriver.com

Barges on the Mississippi River offer spectacular fireworks choreographed in time to stirring patriotic music on Independence Day (July 4).

5 Satchmo Summerfest

504-522-5730 ■ www.fqfi.org

In early August each year one of the city's favorite sons, Louis "Satchmo" Armstrong, is honored with a festival in his name. One of the pre-eminent jazz musicians of the 20th century, Armstrong is heralded with live jazz, seminars, and all-day partying.

Celebrations at Satchmo Summerfest

6 Creole Tomato Festival

Tomatoes have long been an essential crop in Louisiana. Every June, the French Market *(see p90)* hosts a festival dedicated to this fruit with cooking demos, art exhibits, music and dancing, as well as the crowning of the Tomato Queen.

7 Jazz and Heritage Festival

504-410-4100 ▪ www.nojazzfest.com

Covering two weekends in April and May, the locally dubbed "Jazz Fest" offers top performers from all over the world in jazz, gospel, Cajun, R&B, zydeco (Louisiana Creole Blues and R&B), blues, rock, funk, African, and Latin music. Look for local crafts-men displaying their wares and foods.

8 Southern Decadence

www.southerndecadence.net

One of the largest gay and lesbian events in the U.S. takes place in the French Quarter every September. The weekend includes a huge costume parade, drag shows, parties, and more.

9 Essence Festival

www.essence. com/festival

African-American culture is celebrated on the Independence Day weekend every year with the Essence Festival. The program showcases big-name performers, African-American artists, writers, craftsmen, culinary artists, and others.

Essence Festival singer

10 Christmas

504-522-5730
▪ **www.fqfi.org**

Christmas is celebrated across New Orleans with a packed schedule of events: concerts at St. Louis Cathedral, gospel performances, Christmas carols in Jackson Square, and special menus at French Quarter restaurants.

TOP 10 OTHER FESTIVALS AND EVENTS

Halloween New Orleans

1 Tennessee Williams Literary Festival
Held in late March, the festival includes panel discussions, theater, and food.

2 Ponchatoula Strawberry Festival
A short drive from New Orleans, Ponchatoula hosts a festival featuring music, games, strawberry-eating, and cooking contests every April.

3 Greek Festival
This May event features live Greek music, authentic cuisine, a marketplace, and family-friendly activities.

4 Shakespeare Festival
The Bard is honored annually (May–Jul) at Tulane University with performances of his most famous works *(see p50)*.

5 Tales of the Cocktail
The history and culture of the cocktail is the centerpiece of this annual July event.

6 White Linen Night
White linen attire is worn during this annual August street party, held in the city's Warehouse District.

7 New Orleans Bike Week
Bikers gather in Armstrong Park in September for a weekend of food, rides, and live music.

8 Halloween New Orleans™
Every Halloween, the gay community sponsors a party weekend to benefit Lazarus House, an AIDS hospice.

9 Voodoo Music Festival
A Halloween weekend of rock, jazz, and hip hop held every year at New Orleans City Park *(see pp16–17)*.

10 Po-Boy Festival
Celebrate the ubiquitous po'boy with live music at this Oak Street festival, on the third Sunday of October.

TOP 10 Excursions and Day Trips

Oak trees in front of the Oak Alley Plantation

1 Oak Alley Plantation

MAP B2 ■ 3645 Highway 18, Vacherie ■ 225-265-2151 ■ 9am–4:30pm Mon–Fri, 9am–5pm Sat–Sun ■ Adm ■ www.oakalleyplantation.com

The setting for many major movies and television shows, Oak Alley is a striking plantation property. A canopy of giant oak trees forms an impressive avenue that leads to a Greek Revival-style mansion.

2 St. Martin's Parish

■ www.cajuncountry.org

A trip to Louisiana would not be complete without a day spent in Cajun Country. Located in the Atchafalaya Basin, St. Martin's Parish and its surrounding towns form part of a national heritage area. A little over two hours' drive west of New Orleans, this region is rich in history and is home to authentic Cajun and Creole cuisine.

3 St. Martinville

MAP A1 ■ www.stmartin ville.org

With only 7,000 residents, St. Martinville retains its small-town flavor and Southern charm. Every February, the town hosts La Grande Boucherie des Cajuns, which celebrates Cajun culture with feasting and games. The town is also home to an African-American museum, which traces the history of slavery in the region.

4 Rosedown

MAP A1 ■ 12501 Highway 10, St. Francisville ■ 225-635-3332 ■ 9am–5pm daily ■ Adm ■ www.crt.state.la.us

The Rosedown Plantation is distinguished by its sprawling formal gardens, which protect a variety of rare plants. This area is preserved as a historic site by the state.

⑤ Houmas House Plantation and Gardens

MAP B1 ▪ 40136 Highway 942, Darrow ▪ 225-473-9380 ▪ 9am–5pm Mon–Tue, 9am–8pm Wed–Sun ▪ Adm ▪ www.houmashouse.com

This beautiful property, dating back to the mid-18th century, was meticulously restored in 2003 by current owner, Kevin Kelly. The Greek Revival mansion is surrounded by lush landscaped grounds. The gift shop, which stocks classic New Orleans memorabilia and rare books, is a highlight, as is the Latil's Landing Restaurant, which serves traditional Louisiana cuisine.

A traditional property in Lafayette

Houmas House Plantation

⑥ River Road

MAP B2

Often called the Great River Road, this stretch between New Orleans and Baton Rouge is home to some grand, carefully preserved plantation houses. Many of these mansions are open to the public for tours.

⑦ Baton Rouge

MAP B1 ▪ www.visit batonrouge.com

The capital city of Louisiana is worth the hour-long drive from New Orleans. Baton Rouge is a thriving metropolis with great dining and a bustling nightlife. Visitors can also enjoy boat tours of the river, swamp tours, river-boat casinos, and museums, and visit beautiful vineyards.

A statue in St. Francisville

⑧ Lafayette

MAP A1 ▪ www.lafayette travel.com

Although it is a four-hour drive from New Orleans, Lafayette is a popular weekend getaway. Located in the heart of Cajun Country, this city has a very distinct culture and offers visitors many attractions, including eclectic local cuisine, a national park, and a buzzing nightlife.

⑨ Biloxi

www.biloxi.ms.us

An hour's drive from New Orleans, this once-sleepy town has developed into the casino capital of the Gulf Coast. Today, high-rise hotels, big-name entertainers, and flashy casinos are the big draw, not to mention the lovely beaches and exquisite homes and condominiums. The town also offers some of the best sport fishing in the region, and is famous for its delicious seafood.

⑩ St. Francisville

MAP A1

▪ www.stfrancisville.us

Time stands still in this small and elegant town, with its historic mansions and gorgeous 19th-century gardens. Lovely bed and breakfasts, restaurants, art galleries, and specialty shops are the attractions of this typical Southern town.

New Orleans
Area by Area

The New Orleans skyline at night

🔟 Garden District and Uptown

Developed on former plantation land, uptown New Orleans extends over a large part of the city and was founded by the settlers who built commercial properties and houses here. The Garden District was established in 1832 on the Livaudais Plantation, where wealthy merchants, bankers, and planters built grand mansions surrounded by lush gardens, giving the area its name. This neighborhood is distinguished by its beautiful landscaping and provides a retreat from the urban cityscape. A great way to experience these districts is by taking a streetcar ride from the Central Business District to the top of uptown. A large part of the Garden District is a National Historic Landmark District, and visitors can explore the parks, historic buildings, and quaint antiques shops of this neighborhood entirely on foot.

Majestic yellow tiger at Audubon Zoo

GARDEN DISTRICT AND UPTOWN

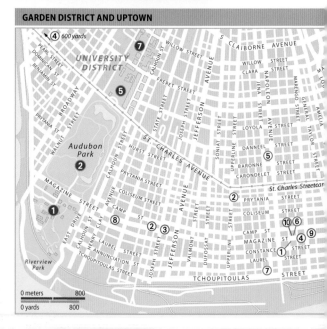

A bucolic scene at a lakeside pavilion in Audubon Park

1 Audubon Zoo

This local treasure is home to a large number of animals from all over the globe and is dedicated to preserving the various species in its care. The emphasis is on interactive and hands-on exhibits, including a children's petting zoo and up-close animal-feeding experiences. Although the zoo's focus is on children's attractions, the overall experience is so enjoyable that it appeals to visitors of all age groups (see pp18–19).

2 Audubon Park

MAP A5 ▪ 6500 Magazine St ▪ 504-861-2537 ▪ www. audubonnatureinstitute.org

With its jogging paths, elegant fountains, Audubon golf course, and zoo, Audubon Park is the centerpiece of the uptown area. The park covers a broad area, from the Mississippi River to St. Charles Avenue. Named for wildlife painter John James Audubon, it is a favorite haunt of local bird-watchers, who are likely to see egrets and several species of duck, among others. A golf clubhouse offers refreshments.

The iconic St. Charles Streetcar

3 St. Charles Streetcar

MAP B5 ▪ 504-827-8300 ▪ Fare $1.25 ▪ www.norta.com

Streetcars are as much a part of the city's character as its architecture, and the St. Charles streetcar is the most famous. The vintage green tram runs for 7 miles (11 km) along St. Charles Avenue, from downtown Canal Street to uptown Carrollton Avenue, through the Central Business District. It has featured in movies, paintings, and novels.

1 **Top 10 Sights**
see pp72–5

1 **Places to Eat**
see p77

1 **Shopping**
see p76

Cornstalk fence at Colonel Short's Villa

4 Colonel Short's Villa
MAP H5 ■ 1448 4th St

Built in 1859 for Colonel Robert Short of Kentucky, this is one of the most stunning historic homes in the Garden District. Designed by architect Henry Howard, the house is known for its cornstalk fence and is a favorite stop on walking tours.

5 Loyola University
MAP B5 ■ 6363 St. Charles Ave
■ 504-865-3240 ■ www.loyno.edu

A Jesuit institution that was declared a university in 1912, Loyola University is spread over two campuses on either side of St. Charles Avenue. With nearly 3,000 students, this is one of the largest private Catholic universities in the South. It offers degrees in many academic disciplines and is also home to the well-respected Thelonious Monk Institute of Jazz Performance. Loyola's imposing Tudor-Gothic architecture is symbolized by the Marquette Hall, one of the grandest buildings on campus.

Marquette Hall at Loyola University

6 Toby's Corner
MAP H5 ■ 2340 Prytania St

A stroll through the Garden District reveals a proliferation of houses built in the Greek-Revival style. Among these is Toby's Corner, built around 1838 and believed to be the oldest house in the city. Named for wealthy merchant Thomas Toby and striking in its simplicity, this suburban villa is raised on brick piers in classic Creole style, to allow air to circulate underneath and to avoid flooding. The grounds also have an interesting fountain fashioned out of a large sugar kettle.

7 Tulane University
MAP B5 ■ 6823 St. Charles Ave
■ 504-865-5000 ■ www.tulane.edu
■ St. Charles streetcar

Often called the "Harvard of the South," Tulane University is a private institution that dates back to the early 1800s. Consistently ranked among the top 50 educational institutions in the U.S., the university is easily identified from St. Charles Avenue by the Romanesque Gibson Hall, constructed in 1894.

8 Robinson House
MAP H5 ■ 1415 3rd St

Robinson House was the first house in New Orleans to feature indoor plumbing. Architect Henry Howard constructed a roof that served as a cistern. Gravity pushed the water down, providing adequate water pressure indoors. Also unique to this home is the Italian villa-style architecture, not commonly found in the South. Another original feature is the fact that the side of the house faces the street.

LOYOLA

GARDEN DISTRICT ARCHITECTURE

Three architectural styles dominate the Garden District area. Double-gallery houses are two-story structures with front-facing galleries on each level; 19th-century town houses are narrow three-story buildings with balconies on the second floor; and the raised center-hall cottages are one-and-a-half-story structures resting on brick piers.

⑨ Briggs-Staub House

MAP H5 ■ 2605 Prytania St

Briggs-Staub House was built in 1849 for Londoner Charles Briggs, who insisted that his home be referred to as a "Gothic Cottage." He appointed architect James Gallier Sr. to design his home. The style was adhered to on the exterior, but, inside, the rooms are larger than one would expect to find in a typical Gothic-Revival house.

Gothic-Revival Briggs-Staub House

⑩ Lafayette Cemetery

MAP H5 ■ 1400 Washington Ave ■ 504-566-5011 ■ 7am–2:30pm Mon–Fri, 7am–12pm Sat ■ Adm for tours ■ www.lafayettecemetery.org

New Orleans is technically below sea level, so its citizens are buried in above-ground tombs and vaults. This walled cemetery was laid out in 1833, its lavish tombs decorated in accordance with the ornate architecture of the Garden District. The best way to see the cemetery and learn about its rich history is through a guided tour (Mon, Wed, Fri, and Sat).

A WALK AROUND THE GARDEN DISTRICT

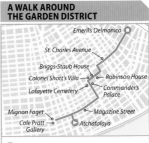

▶ MORNING

Start your day with poached eggs, crab cakes, and fried green tomatoes at **Atchafalaya** (see p77), a popular place serving creative Louisiana cuisine. Next, head northwest to Magazine Street, which has some of the city's best antiques shops and galleries. Browse artworks in a lovely minimalist space at the **Cole Pratt Gallery** (see p76), then step into **Mignon Faget** (see p76), opposite, to admire beautifully handcrafted jewelry. Explore the multitude of tempting stores as you wander down the street to the heart of the Garden District. Bounded by Magazine Street and Louisiana, Charles, and Jackson avenues, this historic neighborhood is one of the city's most charming. Make sure you join a tour of the district or of **Lafayette Cemetery** – the guides will help bring the area to life.

AFTERNOON

After the tour, head to **Commander's Palace** (see p77) for lunch. Be sure to try the signature turtle soup and Creole bread pudding soufflé. After lunch, stroll around the area, admiring its grand mansions, including **Colonel Short's Villa**, **Robinson House**, and **Briggs-Staub House**. Then head toward St. Charles Avenue. Admire the famous **St. Charles streetcar** (see p73) and take in the grand facades of the buildings on this street as you walk to **Emeril's Delmonico** (see p77) for cocktails and a selection of small plates.

See map on pp72–3 ←

Shopping

1 Cole Pratt Gallery
MAP C6 ▪ 3800 Magazine St
▪ 504-891-6789 ▪ www.colepratt
gallery.com

This contemporary fine art gallery specializes in Southern artists. The works are displayed in an elegant minimalist space.

Contemporary art at Cole Pratt Gallery

2 Blue Frog Chocolates
MAP B6 ▪ 5707 Magazine St
▪ 504-269-5707

A chocoholic's delight, Blue Frog boasts an exotic array of individual gourmet candies, cocoa, truffles, bonbons, and sauces, as well as special gift baskets and party trays.

3 Hazelnut
MAP B6 ▪ 5515 Magazine St
▪ 504-891-2424

This interior design store is worth a trip for visitors, as it also sells a range of gifts that you won't find elsewhere in town. You may also catch one of the owners, *Mad Men* star Bryan Batt.

4 Villa Vici
MAP C6 ▪ 4112
Magazine St ▪ 504-899-2931

Well-known interior designer Vikki Leftwich offers innovative lighting, avant-garde furniture, and fine fabrics at her store. This is a great one-stop shop for home decor.

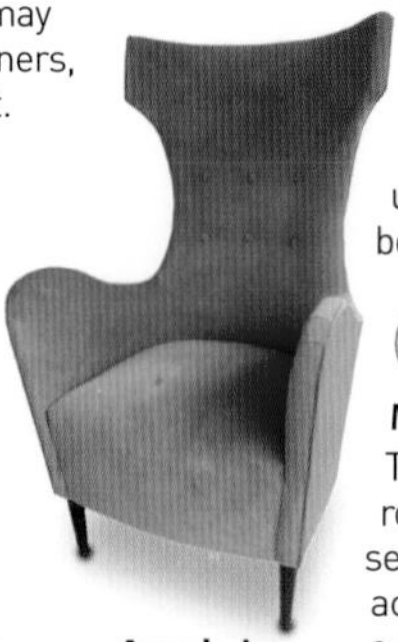

Armchair from Villa Vici

5 Renaissance Shop
MAP J5 ▪ 2104 Magazine St
▪ 504-525-8568

Fine antique reproductions, expert upholstery, and meticulous furniture repair are this shop's specialties.

6 Belladonna Day Spa and Retail Therapy
MAP H6 ▪ 2900 Magazine St
▪ 504-891-4393

This two-story space houses an elegant personal-care and home accessories store on the ground floor and a world-class spa upstairs.

7 Mignon Faget
MAP C6 ▪ 3801 Magazine St
▪ 504-891-2005

An upscale designer jewelry store, Mignon Faget creates beautiful custom-created and specially hand-crafted pieces inspired by New Orleans culture and landscapes.

8 Perlis
MAP B6 ▪ 6070 Magazine St
▪ 504-895-8661

Since 1939, Perlis has been the clothier of choice for many New Orleans families. The store offers casual wear for men, women, and children. It also has a rental and sales division for formal wear.

9 Weinstein's, Inc.
MAP C6 ▪ 4011 Magazine St
▪ 504-895-6278

Weinstein's stocks fine European fashion items for women and an array of upscale designer brands for both men and women.

10 Bella and Harlow
MAP C6 ▪ 4221
Magazine St ▪ 504-324-4531

This chic boutique has a rotating selection of stylish, seasonal dresses, skirts, and accessories. The owner has a great eye for desirable lines at affordable prices.

Places to Eat

PRICE CATEGORIES

For a three-course meal for one, with half a bottle of wine (or equivalent meal), taxes, and extra charges.

$ under $25 $$ $25–$50 $$$ over $50

1 **La Petite Grocery**
MAP C6 ■ 4238 Magazine St
■ 504-891-3377 ■ $$$

Chef and owner Justin Devillier took over after helping to rebuild this elegant restaurant post-Hurricane Katrina. New Orleans dishes with a modern twist include blue crab beignets.

2 **Upperline Restaurant**
MAP C6 ■ 1413 Upperline St
■ 504-891-9822 ■ $$$

A massive art collection is on display here. Do not miss the sensational fried green tomatoes served with shrimp rémoulade.

3 **Coquette**
MAP H6 ■ 2800 Magazine St
■ 504-265-0421 ■ $$$

With a menu focusing on farm-to-table cuisine, Coquette looks like a chic Parisian bistro. All items are offered in both small plate and entrée size. The roasted oysters and smoked catfish are excellent.

4 **Brigtsen's**
MAP A4 ■ 723 Dante St
■ 504-861-7610 ■ $$$

Intimate dining rooms decorated with murals make this place a romantic uptown choice. Housed in a Victorian Creole cottage, Brigtsen's serves renowned gumbo and seafood.

5 **Pascal's Manale**
MAP C5 ■ 1838 Napoleon Ave
■ 504-895-4877 ■ $$$

The barbecued shrimp, an iconic local favorite, is a specialty at Pascal's Manale, opened in 1913. Today, the restaurant still uses the same recipe it devised in the 1950s. It also offers other seafood and Italian dishes.

6 **Shaya**
MAP C6 ■ 4213 Magazine St
■ 504-891-4213 ■ $$$

Simple Mediterranean and Israeli dishes, such as hummus and babaganoush, are prepared elegantly and with superb ingredients.

7 **Dick and Jenny's**
MAP C6 ■ 4501 Tchoupitoulas St
■ 504-894-9880 ■ $$$

Home-cooked meals and luscious calorific desserts, such as the Bananas Foster double cream pie, are the specialties of this place.

8 **Commander's Palace**
MAP H5 ■ 1403 Washington Ave ■ 504-899-8221 ■ $$$

This historic restaurant is the grande dame of New Orleans fine dining. Creole cuisine at its very best.

Elegant room at Emeril's Delmonico

9 **Emeril's Delmonico**
MAP R2 ■ 1300 St. Charles Ave
■ 504-525-4937 ■ $$$

At the most upscale of Emeril's chain of restaurants, diners can sample Chef Anthony Scanio's modern spin on Creole cuisine.

10 **Atchafalaya**
MAP G6 ■ 901 Louisiana Ave
■ 504-891-9626 ■ $$$

The Bloody Mary bar draws crowds to brunch. Dinner choices include shrimp and grits, and duck hash.

See map on pp72–3

TOP 10 CBD and Warehouse District

The hustle and bustle that surrounds daily activity in the downtown area extends all the way through the Warehouse and Central Business districts (CBD). Like that of any other major American city, New Orleans' downtown is a hub of commerce, entertainment, dining, and shopping. But what distinguishes this area is the large concentration of citizens who live here, as well as the number of historic 19th-century buildings that exist in between the profusion of newer structures. Today, many of the old warehouses in these neighborhoods have been converted into stylish spaces housing jazz bars, restaurants, hotels, galleries, and museums.

CBD AND WAREHOUSE DISTRICT

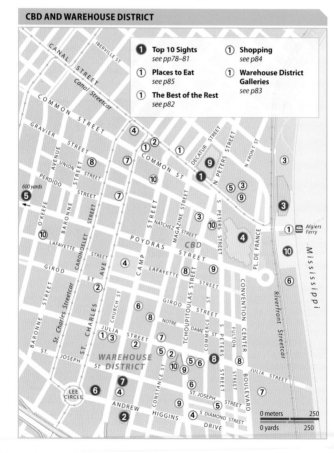

1 Top 10 Sights *see pp78–81*	**1** Shopping *see p84*
1 Places to Eat *see p85*	**1** Warehouse District Galleries *see p83*
1 The Best of the Rest *see p82*	

Canal Street, the main boulevard in New Orleans' downtown area

1 Canal Street

This historic road originally divided old New Orleans into the French and American parts. Named for a proposed canal that was never built, it is the most in-demand spot to watch the Mardi Gras parade, and is lined with restaurants, stores, and luxury hotels. The Canal streetcar is a good way to explore the sights along the length of this road (see pp36–7).

2 The National World War II Museum

MAP Q3 ■ 945 Magazine St ■ 504-528-1944 ■ 9am–5pm daily ■ Adm ■ www.nationalww2museum.org

Boasting a large collection of World War II memorabilia, this museum was created to honor all the Americans who contributed to the war effort. Take the "Behind the Lines Tour," a fascinating visit to the museum's vault with a curator.

3 Audubon Aquarium of the Americas

Held to be the finest of its kind in the country, this aquarium is housed in an ultra-modern building on the banks of the Mississippi. It has three levels of displays of live creatures that inhabit the sea. From the entertaining penguin colony to the huge array of sharks and walk-through underwater tunnel, the aquarium appeals to visitors of all ages. On arrival, be sure to check out the timing of animal feedings for that day (see pp20–21).

4 Harrah's New Orleans Casino

Covering an area of 115,000 sq ft (10,684 sq m), Harrah's tempts visitors with entertainment options ranging from gambling to fine dining. The casino boasts more than 2,000 slot machines, and has games such as roulette, baccarat, and poker on more than 100 tables. It also houses the upscale Besh Steak House, the stylish cocktail lounge Masquerade, with an ice bar, a lavish buffet restaurant, and several smaller restaurants (see p36).

Harrah's New Orleans Casino

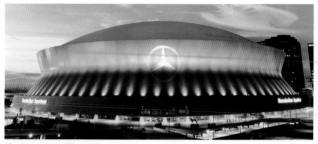

The imposing silhouette of the Mercedes-Benz Superdome

⑤ Mercedes-Benz Superdome

MAP N1 ■ Sugarbowl Drive ■ 504-587-3822 ■ Call for timings ■ Adm ■ www.mbsuperdome.com

This saucer-shaped landmark seating more than 70,000 people is home to the local football team, the Saints. However, the Mercedes-Benz Superdome is much more than just a sports venue: it also hosts major conventions, exhibitions, car shows, and rock concerts.

Ogden Museum of Southern Art

⑥ Ogden Museum of Southern Art

MAP Q3 ■ 925 Camp St ■ 504-539-9600 ■ 10am–5pm Wed–Mon, 10am–8pm Thu ■ Adm ■ www.ogdenmuseum.org

This multilevel building with an industrial feel houses the finest and most diverse collection of Southern art in the U.S. A substantial part of businessman Roger Ogden's huge collection was donated to create this museum, which features everything from folk art to contemporary pieces.

⑦ Contemporary Arts Center New Orleans

MAP Q3 ■ 900 Camp St. ■ 504-528-3805 ■ 11am–4pm Wed–Sun ■ Adm ■ www.cacno.org

Formed in 1976, the Contemporary Arts Center (CAC) was one of the earliest art addresses in the entire Warehouse District. The cavernous building has been refashioned into a workspace for artists, exhibitions, and theater. Although the focus is on visual arts, educational programs and performing arts are highlights too.

⑧ Julia Street

MAP Q3

One of the main streets in the Warehouse District, Julia Street features some of the city's most appealing historic architecture and is New Orleans' gallery neighborhood. The annual White Linen Night street party is hosted here in August – people can browse through art, eat and drink, and enjoy live music.

CANAL STREET: THE FIRST NEUTRAL GROUND

With three traffic lanes, a streetcar, and a bus lane, Canal Street is one of the widest boulevards in the world. The term "neutral ground" originated here in the 1800s, when Anglo-Americans took up residence in the city, and the median strip became the place to settle disputes.

9 Audubon Butterfly Garden and Insectarium

The city's old U.S. Custom House, on the edge of the French Quarter, has been transformed into a museum devoted to all kinds of bugs. Visitors are treated to up-close and personal live insect encounters. Experience being shrunk to bug size when surrounded by the huge exhibits in the Life Underground display, discover the mating and reproduction cycles of insects in the Metamorphosis exhibit, journey through the Louisiana Swamp, or enjoy the tranquility of a butterfly garden and watch hundreds of the winged creatures flit about. Do not miss the cutting-edge insect cuisine. The less intrepid visitor can enjoy an ordinary burger at the Tiny Termite Café with bug-inspired decor (see p37).

A resident at Audubon Insectarium

10 Spanish Plaza

On the Mississippi Riverfront, the Spanish Plaza, with its large central fountain and colorful tiles, is a place where visitors can relax and enjoy a view of the river. It is the starting point for the Creole Queen cruise, and also hosts outdoor concerts and parties (see p23).

Relaxing by the fountain at Spanish Plaza

A WALK AROUND THE WAREHOUSE DISTRICT

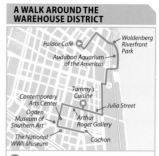

▶ MORNING

Have a breakfast of shrimp and grits or crabmeat cheesecake at the **Palace Café** (see p85) on Canal Street, then make your way to the **Woldenberg Riverfront Park** (see p22), a lovely green area with contemporary sculpture and a view of the river. Next to the park, to the south, is the **Audubon Aquarium of the Americas** (see pp20–21), which is fun to explore. Then walk a few blocks south to **Julia Street** to admire its quaint architecture and plethora of art galleries. Stop by the nationally acclaimed **Arthur Roger Gallery** (see p83), the pinnacle of the local arts scene. Browse and shop at the street's many boutiques before making your way to the **National World War II Museum** (see p79) to see its collection of war memorabilia. Afterward, take a break for a Cajun-inspired lunch of fried alligator or chicken and andouille gumbo at **Cochon** (see p85).

AFTERNOON

Walk back past the National World War II Museum to the **Ogden Museum of Southern Art** and the **Contemporary Arts Center New Orleans** for more visual stimuli and fantastic pieces of art. End your day of culture and art at **Tommy's Cuisine** (746 Tchoupitoulas St.; 504-581-1103; closed Mon), with its Creole delicacies and great collection of wines. Later, make your way back to the Mississippi Riverfront to end your day with one of New Orleans' spectacular sunsets.

See map on p78

The Best of the Rest

Algiers Ferry on the Mississippi

1 Algiers Ferry
MAP P5 ▪ 6am–midnight ▪ Adm from Algiers Point; free from Canal St

Visitors can take a ferry ride to experience the city from the river. This route starts from the foot of Canal Street and ends at the historic Algiers Point.

2 Louisiana Children's Museum
MAP Q4 ▪ 420 Julia St ▪ 504-523-1357 ▪ 9:30am–5pm Mon–Sat, noon–5pm Sun ▪ www.lcm.org

All the displays here are interactive and educational, with monthly special events and visiting exhibits.

3 Woldenberg Riverfront Park
The lovely green area along the banks of the Mississippi River is perfect for biking, jogging, or just spending a lazy afternoon. The park hosts festivals and events throughout the year (see p22).

4 Lafayette Square
MAP P3 ▪ S. Maestri St

A green space hiding within the urban surrounds of the CBD, Lafayette Square is an oasis of tranquility. It also hosts a popular program of free summer concerts known as Wednesdays at the Square.

5 The Howlin' Wolf
One of the few live music venues in the Warehouse District, The Howlin' Wolf hosts rock, jazz, and blues concerts. It has a back room (the Den) for smaller gigs and comedy (see p52).

6 St. Patrick's Church
MAP P3 ▪ 724 Camp St ▪ 504-525-4413 ▪ Timings vary ▪ www.oldstpatricks.org

This Gothic-style church is a National Historic Landmark and an elegant reminder of old New Orleans.

7 Ernest N. Morial Convention Center
One of the largest convention centers in the country, this building boasts state-of-the-art technology (see p23).

8 Mulate's Cajun Restaurant and Dance Hall
MAP Q4 ▪ 201 Julia St ▪ 504-522-1492

Enjoy authentic Cajun food and lively Cajun music, plus dancing lessons for first timers. Do not miss the excellent crabmeat au gratin.

9 Preservation Resource Center
MAP Q4 ▪ 923 Tchoupitoulas St ▪ 504-581-7032 ▪ 9am–5pm Mon–Fri ▪ www.prcno.org

A nonprofit organization, this aims to preserve the historic neighborhoods and develop the resources of the city.

10 Loa
MAP N3 ▪ 221 Camp St ▪ 504-553-9550 ▪ www.ihhotel.com

This shadowy, voodoo-themed bar in the International House Hotel (see p116) offers boutique wines and an array of cocktails.

Warehouse District Galleries

1 **George Schmidt Gallery**
MAP Q3 ▪ 626 Julia St ▪ 504-592-0206 ▪ 12:30–4:30pm Tue–Sat ▪ www.georgeschmidt.com
George Schmidt is known for his pieces documenting the history of New Orleans. The gallery exclusively showcases his work.

2 **Callan Contemporary**
MAP Q3 ▪ 518 Julia St ▪ 504-525-0518 ▪ 10am–5pm Tue–Sat ▪ www.callancontemporary.com
Clean and minimalist, this gallery is home to around 25 of the country's most exciting artists.

3 **Steve Martin Fine Art**
MAP Q3 ▪ 624 Julia St ▪ 504- 566-1390 ▪ 10am–6pm daily ▪ www.stevemartinfineart.com
Internationally recognized, this gallery displays works across various genres.

4 **Contemporary Arts Center New Orleans**
The CAC is dedicated to promoting cutting-edge and even experimental art. Both local and national artists exhibit their works here (see p80).

5 **Arthur Roger Gallery**
MAP Q3 ▪ 432 & 434 Julia St ▪ 504-522-1999 ▪ 10am–5pm Tue–Sat ▪ www.arthurroger gallery.com
Established in 1978 by Arthur Roger, a world-famous purveyor of fine art, this gallery is one of the most high-profile art spaces in the city.

Exhibition in the Arthur Roger Gallery

6 **LeMieux Galleries**
MAP Q4 ▪ 332 Julia St ▪ 504-522-5988 ▪ 10am–6pm Mon–Sat ▪ www.lemieuxgalleries.com
Artists from Louisiana and the rest of the Gulf Coast are the focal point of this contemporary gallery.

Contact Tracing, LeMieux Galleries

7 **Octavia Art Gallery**
MAP Q3 ▪ 454 Julia St ▪ 504-309-4249 ▪ 10am–6pm Tue–Sat ▪ www.octaviaartgallery.com
This gallery displays the work of both emerging and established international contemporary artists.

8 **New Orleans Glassworks**
MAP P3 ▪ 727 Magazine St ▪ 504-529-7279 ▪ 10am–5pm Mon–Sat ▪ www.neworleansglassworks.com
Around 250 artists showcase glass art, sculpture, and printmaking here.

9 **Soren Christensen Gallery**
MAP Q4 ▪ 400 Julia St ▪ 504-569-9501 ▪ 10am–5:30pm Tue–Fri, 11am–5pm Sat ▪ www.sorengallery.com
Sculptures, paintings, and photographs focussing on Southern art are displayed in a bright space.

10 **Jonathan Ferrara Gallery**
MAP Q4 ▪ 400 Julia St ▪ 504-522-5471 ▪ 10am–5pm Mon–Sat ▪ www.jonathanferraragallery.com
This gallery features contemporary works by regional and international artists, as well as new talent.

See map on p78

Shopping

Meyer the Hatter
MAP N3 ▪ 120 St. Charles Ave
▪ 504-525-1048

This third-generation store features quality headwear for men in classic, contemporary, and trendy designs.

2 Rubensteins
Owned by the same family since 1924, Rubensteins is regarded as the finest men's clothing store in the city. It has also started stocking stylish womenswear (see p37).

Shops at Canal Place
A luxury hotel, theaters, and a three-level shopping center with upscale retailers such as Saks Fifth Avenue and Brooks Brothers make up this complex (see p36).

4 Adler's Jewelry
MAP M3 ▪ 722 Canal St ▪ 504-523-5292

Considered one of the finest jewelry retailers in town, Adler's is famous for its custom-designed pieces.

5 Jack Sutton Fine Jewelry
MAP N4 ▪ 365 Canal St ▪ 504-522-8080

Elegant jewelry, ready-to-wear designs, as well as custom pieces are on offer at this high-end store.

6 The Outlet Collection at Riverwalk
This complex houses shops, bars, galleries, restaurants, and other entertainment venues (see p23).

7 Stella Jones Gallery
MAP N3 ▪ 210 St. Charles Ave
▪ 504-568-9050

This lovely exhibition space for African-American artists presents a diverse collection of works. Look out for talks and lectures.

8 The Watch and Clock Shop
MAP N3 ▪ 824 Gravier St ▪ 504-525-3961

Specializing in antiques, this store is dedicated to stylish timepieces. Ask to see the upstairs showroom for the most exclusive items. The store also offers repairs.

9 Ann Taylor
MAP N4 ▪ 333 Canal St
▪ 504-529-2306

Featuring classic American designs for women, Ann Taylor stores offer mix-and-match separates, stylish accessories, and fashionable shoes.

10 Southern Costume Company
MAP P3 ▪ 951 Lafayette St ▪ 504-523-4333

If you're visiting for Mardi Gras, head to this store selling inventive looks created by local costume designers. Rental options and bespoke costumes are also available.

The Outlet Collection at Riverwalk

Places to Eat

1 Palace Café
MAP N3 ■ 605 Canal St
■ 504-523-1661 ■ $$$

Palace Café serves seafood and
Creole specialties. The white
chocolate bread pudding is excellent.

Palace Café's 19th-century interior

5 Emeril's New Orleans
MAP Q4 ■ 800 Tchoupitoulas St
■ 504-528-9393 ■ $$$

Named for its famous chef, Emeril
Lagasse, this restaurant boasts a
diverse menu including andouille-
crusted drum, a flaky freshwater fish.

6 La Boca
MAP Q4 ■ 870 Tchoupitoulas St
■ 504-525-8205 ■ $$$ ■ Closed Sun

One of the best steakhouses in town,
La Boca offers authentic Argentinian
cuisine, plus a remarkable wine list.

7 Luke
MAP P3 ■ 333 St. Charles Ave
■ 504-378-2840 ■ $$$

Towering plates of oysters, mussels,
and seafood are served at this
European-style brasserie overseen
by local top chef John Besh.

2 Herbsaint
MAP P3 ■ 701 St. Charles Ave
■ 504-524-4114 ■ $$$ ■ Closed Sun

This eatery features Southern
classics such as Muscovy duck leg
confit and dark roux gumbos
(seafood stew flavored with
a dark brown sauce).

3 August
MAP R4 ■ 301
Tchoupitoulas St
■ 504-299-9777 ■ $$$

Chef John Besh's flagship
restaurant offers inno-
vative modern French
cuisine served in an elegant room
by knowledgeable staff.

**Colorful dish
from August**

8 Compère Lapin
MAP P4 ■ 535 Tchoupitoulas St
■ 504-599-2119 ■ $$$

With a menu as diverse
as the city itself, chef
Nina Compton serves
seasonal dishes such
as hot-fired chicken and
roasted banana zeppole.

9 Café Adelaide
MAP P4 ■ 300
Poydras St ■ 504-595-3305 ■ $$$

This artsy fine-dining restaurant
excels in Creole dishes. Try the
praline-crusted pork tenderloin.

4 Cochon
MAP R4 ■ 930 Tchoupitoulas St
■ 504-588-2123 ■ $$$ ■ Closed Sun

The menu in this warehouse-style
eatery is pork-focused, and meat
lovers will love Cochon's take on
Cajun dishes. The boucherie plate
is perfect for sharing with friends.

10 The Grill Room
MAP N3 ■ 300 Gravier St
■ 504-522-1994 ■ $$$

Modern Louisiana cuisine is on
offer at this high-end dining room
in the Windsor Court Hotel.

See map on p78

TOP10 French Quarter

This historic district is the oldest part of the city and was built by Jean-Baptiste Le Moyne de Bienville in 1721. Also known as the Vieux Carré or "the Quarter" to locals, it is a mix of evocative Spanish- and French-influenced architecture, and features a lively nightlife and restaurant scene. The epicenter is Jackson Square, named for President Andrew Jackson, and populated by local artists, musicians, and tarot-card readers. Bourbon Street cuts a lurid swathe through the center with its karaoke bars and strip clubs, while Royal Street provides a cultural contrast with its elegant galleries and antiques shops. Decatur Street runs parallel to the Mississippi River and is home to the bustling French Market, where traders have been active since 1791.

Busking on Royal Street

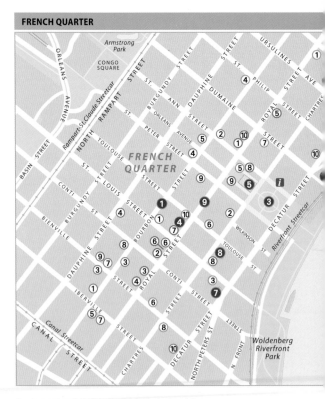

FRENCH QUARTER

Neon-lit Bourbon Street, one of New Orleans' main entertainment hubs

1 Bourbon Street

A hotbed of shops, restaurants, clubs, and other entertainment options, Bourbon Street turns into a pedestrian zone at night, with visitors going from club to club, dancing, drinking, and partying *(see pp32–3)*. Liquor laws allow drinking on the streets, so all the bars serve drinks to go.

2 Old Ursuline Convent

MAP L5 ■ 1100 Chartres St ■ 504-529-3040 ■ Tours: 10am–4pm Tue–Fri (last tour 3:15pm); 9am–3pm Sat (last tour 2:15pm) ■ Adm ■ www.stlouiscathedral.org

Built in 1752, the Old Ursuline Convent is the oldest surviving building in the Mississippi River Valley. Tours of the convent, which was home to the founding Ursuline Sisters, reveal its beautiful hand-crafted cypress staircase, paintings, religious statuary, and bronze busts. The building has operated as an orphanage, a hospital, and a residence hall for bishops.

3 Jackson Square

Originally used for meetings and public executions, Jackson Square is now a beautiful garden. It is adjacent to the St. Louis Cathedral *(see p90)* and the Pontalba Apartment Buildings *(see p27)*, which are the oldest apartments in the country. In the center of the square is a statue of former U.S. president Andrew Jackson, dedicated to his victory at the Battle of New Orleans in 1815. Along the perimeter are restaurants and novelty shops, all facing out to the artists, fortune tellers, palm readers, and jazz musicians who spend their days working in the square *(see pp26–7)*.

0 meters 200
0 yards 200

ESPLANADE AVE
DECATUR ST
N PETERS STREET

⑨

⑥

Mississippi

4 Historic New Orleans Collection

MAP M4 ▪ 533 Royal St ▪ 504-523-4662 ▪ 9:30am–4:30pm Tue–Sat, 10:30am–4:30pm Sun ▪ www.hnoc.org

The history of New Orleans goes back about three centuries, and the Historic New Orleans Collection is the pre-eminent collection of archives on the city, and includes a permanent exhibit on French Quarter history. It began with the donation of a personal collection in 1966, but has since expanded into a state-of-the-art resource center on Louisiana. Today, it also serves as a facility for researchers.

Poster, Historic New Orleans Collection

5 St. Louis Cathedral

MAP L4 ▪ 615 Pere Antoine Alley ▪ 504-525-9585 ▪ Tours: 1–4pm Wed–Sat ▪ www.stlouiscathedral.org

The oldest continuously active Roman Catholic cathedral in the country, St. Louis was originally constructed in 1727, lost to a fire, then rebuilt in the mid-19th century. The breathtaking interior is maintained by the Archdiocese of New Orleans. Behind the church is an elegant garden with an imposing statue of Jesus. In the evening spotlights illuminate the statue, projecting a giant shadow on the back wall of the church, adding to its ambience.

6 The French Market and Lower Decatur Street

MAP L6 ▪ 1235 N. Peters St ▪ 504-596-3420 ▪ www.frenchmarket.org

Located between Decatur Street and the Mississippi, the French Market has been a dedicated market space for more than 200 years. As well as a produce market, there is a flea market here. Lower Decatur Street is a mix of open yards and garages selling antiques and costume items, plus bars, music venues, and restaurants, as well as gift and t-shirt shops.

7 Jean Lafitte National Historical Park Visitor Center

MAP M4 ▪ 419 Decatur St ▪ 504-589-3882 ▪ www.nps.gov ▪ 9am–5pm daily

A great place for a quick lesson on the geography, history, and culture of the Mississippi River Delta region, this park consists of six sites in Louisiana, all offering informative guided tours by park rangers.

8 Chartres Street

MAP M4

Even in the heart of the French Quarter, some streets offer welcome respite from the bustling crowds. Step from the sea of "to-go" cups on Bourbon Street and Royal Street onto Chartres Street (pronounced "charters"), which runs between

St. Louis Cathedral, facing Jackson Square

St. Louis Cathedral and Jackson Square. Browse antiques stores and galleries, sample classic New Orleans cuisine, and admire some of the finest architecture in the French Quarter.

yal Street, popular with shoppers

⑨ Royal Street

This street offers exquisite antiques shops, fine jewelry stores, sophisticated cocktail bars, famous restaurants, and art galleries that attract collectors from all over the world. It also features the French Quarter's grandest mansions. Every afternoon, street musicians and performers entertain visitors (see pp28–31).

⑩ New Orleans Jazz National Historical Park

MAP L5 ▪ 916 N. Peters St ▪ 504-589-4841 ▪ 9am–5pm Tue–Sat ▪ www.nps.gov

Located within Armstrong Park, the New Orleans Jazz National Historical Park honors the city as the birthplace of jazz. The park is home to Perseverance Hall, a rare surviving original jazz dance hall built in 1819, where African-American musicians trained and performed for both white and African-American audiences.

HAUNTED HOTEL

Rumors of ghosts float about the Hotel Monteleone (see p29). Guests and staff have reported doors opening on their own, elevators stopping on the wrong floor, and ghostly images of children. It is on the list of most haunted hotels in the country.

A DAY IN THE FRENCH QUARTER

▶ MORNING

Start your day early and avoid the crowds at **Café du Monde** (see p60), where you can fuel up on café au lait and beignets. From there, walk a few blocks along to the **French Market**, where local farmers will be setting up their produce stalls – you can get first pick at the flea market, which has artworks, jewelry, and souvenirs. There's time to dip into the museum at the **Old U.S. Mint** (see p92) before walking back to **Central Grocery & Deli** (see p95), which has the most famous muffulettas in town. You'll need just a half, or you can split one while people-watching.

EVENING

Head over to **Bourbon Street** (see p89) in the early evening and grab a Sazerac cocktail at the **Bourbon House Restaurant** (see p95), coupled with a dish or two from their famous oyster bar (the happy hour runs 4–6pm). This sets you up nicely for dinner at the historic and atmospheric **Arnaud's** (see p95), famous for its soufflé potatoes. Be sure to check out the Mardi Gras Museum upstairs. After dinner, wander over to the **Chris Owens Club** (see p94), where the oldest performer on Bourbon Street, owner Chris Owens, puts on an electrifying one-woman show. End the night with some traditional jazz at **Fritzel's European Jazz Pub** (see p94), where visitors squeeze in to enjoy some of New Orleans' finest music.

See map on pp88–9

The Best of the Rest

1 Gallier House Museum
James Gallier, Jr. was one of the most prominent 19th-century architects in New Orleans. His elegant Victorian home is now a museum showcasing the architecture of the period *(see p29)*.

2 Beauregard-Keyes House and Garden
MAP L5 ■ 1113 Chartres St ■ 504-523-7257 ■ 10am–3pm Mon–Sat ■ Adm ■ www.bkhouse.org
Built in 1826, this house is named for Confederate general P. G. T. Beauregard and author Frances Parkinson Keyes. It features raised center-hall architecture.

3 Kurt E. Schon, Ltd.
MAP M4 ■ 510 St. Louis St ■ 504-524-5462 ■ 10am–5pm Mon–Fri, 10am–3pm Sat ■ www.kurte schonltd.com
This gallery has been around in the Upper French Quarter for more than 50 years. Spread over five floors, it boasts an impressive collection of 18th- and 19th-century art.

4 Lafitte's Blacksmith Shop Bar
Originally a late-18th-century tavern, Lafitte's Blacksmith Shop is one of the oldest buildings in New Orleans. It is also one of the hottest bars in the city today *(see p32)*.

5 Rodrigue Studio
George Rodrigue became famous for his humorous "Blue Dog" series. His paintings are now serious collector's items *(see p29)*.

6 Michalopoulos
MAP M4 ■ 617 Bienville St ■ 504-558-0505 ■ 10am–6pm Mon–Sat, 11am–6pm Sun ■ www.michalopoulos.com
Colorful, contemporary works by celebrated New Orleans artist James Michalopoulos are displayed here.

7 Madame John's Legacy
MAP L5 ■ 632 Dumaine St ■ 504-568-6968 ■ 10am–4:30pm Tue–Sun ■ www.louisianastatemuseum.org
This authentic 18th-century Creole mansion is one of the finest examples of French colonial architecture in North America.

8 Callan Fine Art
MAP N4 ■ 240 Chartres St ■ 504-524-0025 ■ Call for timings ■ www.callanfineart.com
This is the place for European art from 1830 to 1950 covering the Academic Art style, the American Barbizon style, and modern works.

9 Old U.S. Mint
MAP L6 ■ 400 Esplanade Ave ■ 504-568-6993 ■ 9:30am–4:30pm Tue–Sat ■ Adm ■ www.louisiana statemuseum.org
Part of the Louisiana State Museum, the mint now houses the New Orleans Jazz Museum, with a live performance venue *(see p43)*.

10 Galerie d'Art Français
MAP M4 ■ 541 Royal St ■ 504-581-6925 ■ Call for timings ■ www.neworleansfrenchart.com
An important selection of 20th-century French art, including many Impressionist works, is housed here.

Trendy Lafitte's Blacksmith Shop Bar

Shopping

Intimate Bourbon French Parfums

1 Bourbon French Parfums
MAP L4 ▪ 805 Royal St ▪ 504-522-4480 ▪ www.neworleans
perfume.com
This tiny perfumery has been custom blending lovely fragrances since 1843.

2 The Brass Monkey
MAP M4 ▪ 407 Royal St ▪ 504-561-0688
One of the French Quarter's most eclectic gift shops, the Brass Monkey boasts a large collection of Limoges figu-rines and miniature boxes.

3 Jack Sutton Fine Jewelry
MAP M4 ▪ 315 Royal St ▪ 504-522-0555 ▪ www.jacksutton.com
The city's premier fine jewelry destination offers everything from hip-hop jewelry to diamonds.

4 Royal Antiques
MAP M4 ▪ 309 Royal St ▪ 504-524-7033 ▪ www.royalantiques.com
Known for its fine art and furni-shings, Royal Antiques sells beautiful mirrors, clocks, and lamps.

5 Fifi Mahony's
MAP L5 ▪ 934 Royal St ▪ 504-525-4343
In a town that loves fancy-dress costumes, Fifi Mahony's is the perfect store, stocking party wigs, cosmetics, and unique accessories.

6 Moss Antiques
MAP M4 ▪ 411 Royal St ▪ 504-522-3981 ▪ www.mossantiques.com
A family-owned antiques store, Moss Antiques sells art, china, furniture, and chandeliers, as well as a constantly evolving and diverse inventory of new acquisitions.

7 Fleur de Paris
The only serious millinery store in the South, this popular European-style boutique also offers couture fashion, exquisite jewelry, lingerie, and a collection of elegant beaded handbags (see p29).

Maskarade Mask Shop

8 Maskarade Mask Shop
MAP L4 ▪ 630 St. Ann St ▪ 504-568-1018 ▪ www.themaskstore.com
New Orleanians love masks and this shop provides some wonderfully original ones. They're available to buy all year, not just during Mardi Gras.

9 Faulkner House Books
This small and charming bookstore is a real treat for anyone who loves books. It specializes in rarities, first editions, and works by renowned American authors (see p27).

10 Erzulie's Authentic Voudou
MAP L4 ▪ 807 Royal St ▪ 504-525-2055 ▪ www.erzulies.com
Part retail store and part spiritual and psychic services center, Erzulie's Authentic Voudou is a place with a whole lot of character.

See map on pp88–9 ➤

Nightlife

1 Chris Owens Club
Famous Louisiana singer and dancer Chris Owens wows the crowds with her nightly burlesque performances at this club *(see p32)*.

2 OZ
 MAP L4 ■ 800 Bourbon St ■ 504-593-9491

Located in the gay district, OZ is the premier dance club in the area. There are live shows, and the music carries on till the wee hours.

3 The Jazz Playhouse
Live jazz revues and tasteful burlesque performances take place nightly at this upscale jazz club tucked inside the Royal Sonesta Hotel *(see pp32–3)*.

4 Cat's Meow Karaoke Club
Located in a 19th-century building, this lively karaoke club is a non-stop party, offering its guests playlists covering hundreds of songs *(see p32)*.

5 Fritzel's European Jazz Pub
MAP L4 ■ 733 Bourbon St ■ 504-586-4800

This is one of the few places on Bourbon Street where you can hear authentic New Orleans jazz.

6 One Eyed Jacks
MAP L3 ■ 615 Toulouse St ■ 504-569-8361

Enjoy the eclectic line-up of live music or the dance parties – the most popular is the Thursday night tribute to the 1980s.

7 French 75 Bar
MAP M3 ■ 813 Bienville St ■ 504-523-5433

This small bar is welcoming and sophisticated. Order the signature French 75 cocktail (champagne and brandy) and a plate of soufflé potatoes.

Cocktail from French 75 Bar

8 Famous Door
Since the 1930s, this raucous Bourbon Street club has been providing live entertainment, as well as night-long dancing every day of the week *(see p32)*.

9 Pat O'Brien's
There's a fun atmosphere at this iconic, long-running bar. Guests can keep the tall glass of their "Hurricane" as a souvenir *(see p32)*.

10 House of Blues
MAP N4 ■ 225 Decatur St ■ 504-310-4999

From regional bands and solo acts to internationally acclaimed jazz, rock, and blues performers, the House of Blues is the last word in live music.

A band performing at the legendary House of Blues

Places to Eat

 Galatoire's Restaurant
The crown jewel of Bourbon Street, Galatoire's is a historic spot dating back to 1905, and is one of the few restaurants left that require gentlemen to wear a jacket. It also has the liveliest Friday lunch in town *(see p32)*.

 Sylvain
MAP M4 ▪ 625 Chartres St ▪ 504-265-8123 ▪ $$$

Located in the French Quarter, Sylvain offers a fresh take on local dishes, paired with creative cocktails. There is also a lovely courtyard.

3 G. W. Fins
MAP M3 ▪ 808 Bienville St ▪ 504-581-3467 ▪ $$$

This seafood fine dining restaurant stands out for its distinctive dishes, such as halibut topped with thinly sliced scallops and served with lobster risotto.

 Bayona
MAP M3 ▪ 430 Dauphine St ▪ 504-525-4455 ▪ $$$ ▪ Closed Sun

The flagship restaurant of chef Susan Spicer, this cottage has a lovely courtyard and a fine menu of creative Louisiana classics. Lunch is especially good value.

5 Bourbon House Restaurant
This restaurant boasts an outstanding oyster bar and is renowned for its excellent Creole preparations, such as crabmeat-stuffed Gulf fish *(see p32)*.

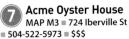 **Brennan's**
MAP M4 ▪ 417 Royal St ▪ 504-525-9711 ▪ $$$

A massive renovation in 2014 restored this iconic eatery to its original 1940s glory. Classic dishes include turtle soup and redfish amandine.

7 Acme Oyster House
MAP M3 ▪ 724 Iberville St ▪ 504-522-5973 ▪ $$$

Enjoy hand-shucked Louisiana oysters, cold on the half shell, or chargrilled with garlic butter.

The bar area at Napoleon House

8 Napoleon House
MAP N4 ▪ 500 Chartres St ▪ 504-524-9752 ▪ $$

Locals and tourists line up for solid po'boy sandwiches, legendary muffulettas, and other Creole classics.

9 Arnaud's
MAP M3 ▪ 813 Bienville St ▪ 504-523-5433 ▪ $$$

An upscale place offering Creole cuisine: try the spicy Shrimp Arnaud. After dinner, visit the Mardi Gras Museum on the second floor.

10 Central Grocery & Deli
MAP N4 ▪ 923 Decatur St ▪ 504-523-1620 ▪ $

This 1906 Italian store with just a few seats has the best muffulettas in town, which were invented right here.

See map on pp88–9 →

🔟 Bywater, Marigny, and Treme

These downtown districts contain a wealth of food, nightlife, and entertainment options. The Marigny and Bywater districts, served by the Rampart-St. Claude Streetcar, continue along the Mississippi's edge from the French Quarter. The Marigny is a leafy area with quirky cafés, musical Frenchmen Street, and a buzzing arts corridor. Hip Bywater is home to visual and performance arts venues, as well as to Crescent Park, while Treme is the oldest African-American

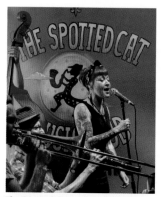

neighborhood in the US and has a proud musical and cultural heritage.

The Spotted Cat on Frenchmen Street

① Frenchmen Street
MAP K6

The Frenchmen in question were leaders of an uprising against Spanish rule after Louisiana was ceded to Spain in 1768, and were executed for their trouble. The street is now the place to enjoy restaurants and a large number of live music clubs, ranging from traditional jazz to reggae to rock. Some of New Orleans' best clubs are here, including The Spotted Cat (see p100). There is often live music in the street itself.

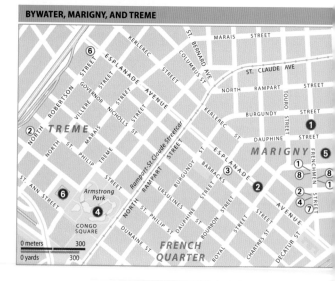

BYWATER, MARIGNY, AND TREME

2 Esplanade Avenue
MAP K5

Separating the French Quarter from the Marigny, Esplanade Avenue stretches from the Mississippi River to New Orleans City Park. It is lined with lovely historical mansions dating back to the 19th century, when it was the address of choice for rich Creole citizens. There are also quaint bistros, cafés, ethnic restaurants, and houses representing most of the architectural styles of the 18th and 19th centuries.

Colorful mansions along Esplanade Avenue

3 Piety Street Bridge
MAP N4 ■ Piety St at Chartres St

This huge, arching bridge at the entrance to Crescent Park (see p98) is constructed out of raw, untreated steel. The corrosive effects are purposely in view, giving it the local nickname of "The Rusty Rainbow." It's a somewhat severe architectural statement, but a memorable one, paying homage to the railways that once ran here and to the industrial heritage of the area.

4 Armstrong Park and Congo Square
MAP K4 & L3 ■ 701 N. Rampart St

Directly across from the French Quarter, the lush Armstrong Park features a statue of New Orleans' favorite son, Louis "Satchmo" Armstrong, at the entrance. The site of jazz concerts and festivals throughout the year, the park is the start point for the Krewe of Barkus dog parade during Mardi Gras. At the southern end of the park lies Congo Square, an open space where slaves and free "people of color" gathered to dance and sing throughout the 19th century, and where the seeds of jazz in the city were sown.

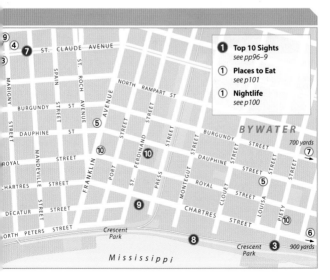

ST. CLAUDE AVENUE
SPAIN STREET
NORTH RAMPART ST
MARIGNY
BURGUNDY STREET
DAUPHINE ST
ROYAL STREET
MANDEVILLE STREET
CHARTRES STREET
DECATUR STREET
NORTH PETERS STREET
ROCH AVENUE
FRANKLIN
PORT
ST. FERDINAND
PRESS
MONTEGUT
BURGUNDY STREET
DAUPHINE STREET
ROYAL STREET
CLOUET STREET
CHARTRES STREET
LOUISA
PIETY
BYWATER
Crescent Park
Mississippi

	Top 10 Sights see pp96–9
	Places to Eat see p101
	Nightlife see p100

700 yards
900 yards

5 Washington Square
MAP K6

An urban park, Washington Square is the site for special events and festivals. The most important of these is the annual Gay Pride Festival. The square is also a great place for a walk or a meal at any of the numerous surrounding restaurants.

6 Mahalia Jackson Theater of the Performing Arts
MAP K3 ■ 1419 Basin St ■ 504-287-0351 ■ Call for timings ■ Adm ■ www.mahaliajacksontheater.com

Named for the acclaimed Queen of Gospel music, Mahalia Jackson, this world-class theater showcases Broadway musicals and diverse performances by famous musicians, comedians, dancers, ballet companies, and more. The highlight of Basin Street, this multilevel theater can seat 2,243 people.

The Mahalia Jackson Theater

7 St. Claude Avenue
MAP K4

The streetcar extension project is the cherry on the cake for the development of the St. Claude corridor. Well-established arts venues such as The AllWays Lounge, Siberia, and HiHo Lounge *(see p100)* have been complemented in recent years by new restaurants, most of which serve dishes that fall outside of the usual Creole offerings. A fringe theater, The Theater at St. Claude, and a high-end food court, St. Roch Market, mean that more and more visitors are now exploring this lively and deserving area.

Aerial view of Crescent Park

8 Crescent Park
MAP N4 ■ 1008 N. Peters St

A green space running between Elysian Fields in the Marigny and Mazant Street in the Bywater, Crescent Park has long stretches of grass and quiet pathways, plus the remnants of an old wharf building. There are spots to sit next to the Mississippi. Thanks to the river's peculiar bends, in some places there are splendid views of the city skyline.

9 New Orleans Centre for Creative Arts (NOCCA)
MAP N4 ■ 2800 Chartres St ■ 504-940-2787 ■ www.nocca.com

Billed as "Louisiana's Arts Conservatory," NOCCA was established to train the city's young talent. Its major disciplines are dance, music, theater, and visual arts, but culinary and cinematic courses are also available. Famous graduates include Harry Connick, Jr., Terence Blanchard, and Wendell

STREETCAR SCENE

A Rampart-St. Claude Streetcar line opened in October 2016, running from the Union Passenger Terminal on Calliope Street to Elysian Fields. New spots are opening up along this stretch all the time, and the line makes exploring Marigny, Bywater, and Treme even easier.

Pierce. The facility arranges occasional student productions, usually around the end of term, which are sometimes open to the public (check online).

10 Marigny Opera House
725 St. Ferdinand St ■ 504-948-9998 ■ www.marignyopera house.org

Many New Orleans venues are former churches, but none is as impressive as this self-proclaimed "church of the arts." The building itself dates back to 1853. In 2011 it was transformed into a venue for classical music, dance, and theater. The Opera House has a strong line in operatic productions and contemporary dance.

Facade of Marigny Opera House

NOSING AROUND THE NEIGHBORHOODS

MORNING

Start the day with a coffee from Mr. Gregory's (806 N Rampart St), just across from **Armstrong Park** (see p97), then go for a stroll around the land-scaped gardens, taking in **Congo Square** (see p97) and paying your respects to the statue of Louis Armstrong. As you exit, head toward the Marigny and walk through the colorful streets to riverside **Crescent Park**, where you can take photos of the New Orleans city skyline. From here, cross the **Piety Street Bridge** (see p97) back to the Bywater – lunch can be a few slices of pizza and a cold local beer at **Pizza Delicious** (see p101). Euclid Records (3301 Chartres St.) and **Dr. Bob's Folk Art** (3027 Chartres St.) are in the vicinity for some post-lunch music and art browsing.

EVENING

After a siesta, take an early evening walk to **Frenchmen Street** (see p96), where you can stop off at **The Spotted Cat** (see p100) for a cocktail and some traditional jazz, or sample some small plates at **The Three Muses** (see p101), where diners are entertained by local musicians. There's also the chance to see some of the city's best artists and impressive crafts at the night-time-only **Frenchmen Art Market** (see p100) before continuing to **St. Claude Avenue**. From here, you'll have a choice of entertainment options – perhaps a DJ set at **HiHo Lounge**, a burlesque show at **AllWays Lounge**, or a rock band at **Siberia** (see p100), where – if you're still hungry – there's a great Slavic kitchen at the back that stays open late into the night.

See map on pp96–7 ←

Nightlife

Frenchmen Art Market, a night-time event where visitors can buy local art

1 Frenchmen Art Market
MAP K6 ■ 619 Frenchmen St ■ 504-941-1149

Grab a cocktail from The Spotted Cat and wander around this night-time market, which sells paintings, sculpture, clothing, and souvenirs.

2 Candlelight Lounge
MAP L2 ■ 925 N. Robertson St ■ 504-571-1201

The best brass bands in the city, including the Treme Brass Band themselves, play at this unassuming but colorful Treme venue.

3 The AllWays Lounge and Theatre
MAP K4 ■ 2240 St. Claude Ave ■ 504-218-5778

Every night has a different vibe at this kitsch venue, from comedy, drag, and burlesque, to folk music.

4 The HiHo Lounge
MAP K4 ■ 2239 St. Claude Ave ■ 504-945-4446

This place has inexpensive bar food and an eclectic mix of events, such as comedy, DJs, and some of the city's most risqué burlesque shows.

5 Lost Love Lounge
MAP M3 ■ 2529 Dauphine St ■ 504-949-2009

This friendly Marigny bar is a great place to watch sports. It has a Vietnamese kitchen in the back.

6 Bacchanal
600 Poland Ave ■ 504-948-9111

This well-stocked wine bar with a huge patio offers live music, plus hot food and cheese plates.

7 Maison
MAP K6 ■ 508 Frenchmen St ■ 504-371-5543

Maison has a respectable menu for laid-back, early evening dinner jazz shows and three music stages for livelier late-night sets.

8 The Spotted Cat
MAP K6 ■ 623 Frenchmen St ■ 504-943-3887

Traditional jazz and swing dancing rule at this lively Frenchmen institution with a packed bar.

8 Siberia
MAP K4 ■ 2227 St. Claude Ave ■ 504-265-8855

Predominantly a heavy rock bar, Siberia also offers some great acoustic sets. The Slavic kitchen is worth seeking out.

10 Mimi's in the Marigny
MAP L5 ■ 2601 Royal St ■ 504-872-9868

Visitors come to this beloved Marigny staple for the lively crowds and pool table, and stay for their wonderful small plates and tapas. There's usually dancing in the upstairs bar.

Places to Eat

1 **Marigny Brasserie**
MAP K6 ▪ 640 Frenchmen St
▪ 504-945-4472 ▪ $$$

This chic and bright restaurant has a seasonal menu where dishes feature fresh, local ingredients.

2 **Praline Connection**
MAP K6 ▪ 542 Frenchmen St
▪ 504-943-3934 ▪ $$$

As well as delicious pralines, this quaint place offers Creole "soul food." Try their seafood stuffed peppers.

3 **Port of Call**
MAP J2 ▪ 838 Esplanade Ave
▪ 504-523-0120 ▪ $$

The lines out of the door pay testament to the enduring popularity of this burger joint.

4 **Three Muses**
MAP K6 ▪ 536 Frenchmen St
▪ 504-252-4801 ▪ $$

Part music venue, part restaurant, Three Muses fills up quickly. Tasty small plates complement the light jazz, while the cocktail list is thought to be among the best downtown.

The leafy patio area at Oxalis

5 **Oxalis**
MAP M3 ▪ 3162 Dauphine St
▪ 504-267-4776 ▪ $$$

This gastro-pub-style eatery in the Bywater serves elevated bar food and a menu of 175 whiskeys.

PRICE CATEGORIES
For a three-course meal for one, with half a bottle of wine (or equivalent meal), taxes, and extra charges.

$ under $25 $$ $25–$50 $$$ over $50

6 **Li'l Dizzy's Café**
MAP J2 ▪ 1500 Esplanade Ave
▪ 504-569-8997 ▪ $

What this place lacks in fanciness, it makes up for with the soul in its Creole menu. Everything is delicious, from the fried chicken and gumbo to the shrimp and grits.

7 **Sneaky Pickle**
MAP K4 ▪ 4017 St. Claude Ave
▪ 504-218-5651 ▪ $$

Good-value nutritious and playful vegan and vegetarian food is the name of the game here, although the occasional meat dish sneakily makes the cut. The daily specials are usually wonderful.

8 **Café Rose Nicaud**
MAP K6 ▪ 632 Frenchmen St
▪ 504-949-3300 ▪ $

Named after a slave who became the first coffee seller in New Orleans, this café is popular with locals for its healthy, fresh Cajun breakfasts and a surprisingly good lunch menu.

9 **Siberia**
MAP K4 ▪ 2227 St. Claude Ave
▪ 504-265-8855 ▪ $

The Slavic menu makes for a delightful change from Southern cuisine, and the pierogi (dumplings) and blinis are prepared just right. The main draw, however, is the fabulous beetburger.

10 **Pizza Delicious**
617 Piety St ▪ 504-676-8482
▪ $$ ▪ Closed Mon

Routinely voted the best pizzeria in the city, this busy place offers a small but adventurous pizza menu. It is complemented by a very good line in pastas, salads, and sides.

See map on pp96–7

TOP 10 Mid-City

Extending from the French Quarter toward Lake Pontchartrain, Mid-City was carved out of a former plantation and is the greenest part of New Orleans. Dominated by the New Orleans City Park and intersected by the major thoroughfares of Canal Street and Esplanade Avenue, Mid-City is a predominantly residential area and is home to the original New Orleans families. Their distinct culture is exemplified by the fact that they have had their own Mardi Gras krewes since 1933. The Canal streetcar winds its way through this lovely neighborhood, which is dotted with cemeteries, canals, parkways, and Creole mansions. Although the area was heavily damaged by Hurricane Katrina, extensive reconstruction work has helped restore much of its delightful original charm.

The bright-red Canal Streetcar

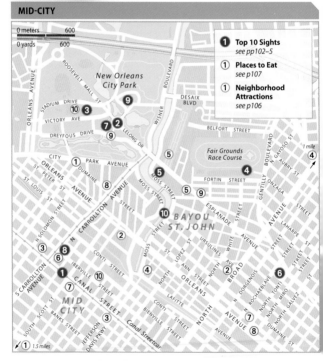

MID-CITY

0 meters 600
0 yards 600

1	**Top 10 Sights** see pp102–5
①	**Places to Eat** see p107
①	**Neighborhood Attractions** see p106

Roosevelt Mall St

New Orleans City Park

Orleans Avenue

Stadium Drive
Victory Ave
Dreyfous Drive

Wisner Boulevard
Desaix Blvd
Belfort Street

Fair Grounds Race Course

City Park Avenue
Orleans Avenue
Dumaine
N Carrollton Avenue
Moss Street
Fortin Street
Gentilly Boulevard
Onzaga St
Gayoso St
Aubry St

1 mile

Esplanade Avenue
Bayou St. John
Harpe Street

St Louis St
St Peter St
N Solomon Street

Conti Street
Moss Street
Ursulines
N Lopez St
N White Street
N Broad Street
Dorgenois Street
Rochablave Street
North Tonti
North Miro
North Galvez

S Carrollton Avenue
Iberville Street
Canal Street
Bienville Street
Lafitte Street
North Orleans Avenue
Conti Street
Dumaine St

South Scott Street
Banks Street
Jefferson Davis Pkwy

MID CITY
Canal Streetcar

1.5 miles

Colorful flowerbeds in bloom at the New Orleans Botanical Garden

1 Canal Streetcar
504-248-3900 ▪ Adm
▪ www.norta.com

This streetcar line, which begins at the Mississippi River, dates back to the mid-19th century. It travels through the CBD and well into Mid-City before coming to a stop at NOMA (see pp12–15). The vintage vehicles are fitted with wooden seats and painted a bright red. Locals use the streetcar as an inexpensive way to commute, whereas visitors find it the best mode of sightseeing, as the streetcar stops at most of the significant sights in Mid-City and travels at a leisurely pace.

2 New Orleans Museum of Art

An architectural and cultural gem in the Mid-City area, the New Orleans Museum of Art (NOMA) showcases ten permanent collections from all over the world, as well as high-profile rotating exhibitions. NOMA also has an active schedule of educational programs, children's programs, and special events that are open to the public. The museum gift shop offers some high-end and unique works of art, jewelry, accessories, and books (see pp12–15).

Sculpture at the New Orleans Museum of Art

3 New Orleans Botanical Garden

Originally known as the City Park Rose Garden, these gardens combine landscaping techniques with art and architecture. Today, more than 2,000 plant varieties can be found here. Mostly cared for by local volunteers, the gardens feature plants and flowers indigenous to Louisiana. Because of the tropical climate in New Orleans, the Botanical Garden showcases its best foliage and flowering plants almost year-round. The adjacent conservatory features a simulated tropical rain forest and a raging waterfall (see p16).

4 Fair Grounds Race Course & Slots
MAP D1 ▪ 1751 Gentilly Blvd
▪ 504-944-5515 ▪ Adm for clubhouse
▪ www.fairgroundsracecourse.com

Founded in 1852, the Fair Grounds are home to the third-oldest continuously running race track in the country as well as over 600 slot machines. The annual races are held from Thanksgiving Day to the end of March. Visitors can watch the races outdoors, or enjoy the comforts of the clubhouse, with fine dining and monitors to keep abreast of events on the track. Fair Grounds hosts the New Orleans Jazz and Heritage Festival (see p67).

A room in the Pitot House Museum

5 Pitot House Museum

MAP J3 ▪ 1440 Moss St ▪ 504-482-0312 ▪ Tours 10am–3pm Wed–Fri, Saturdays by appointment only ▪ Adm ▪ www.pitothouse.org

Built in the late 18th century, Pitot House is a Creole-Colonial-style building on the banks of the Bayou St. John. It has had several owners, including lawyers and nuns, but is named for James Pitot, the first American mayor of New Orleans, who lived here from 1810 to 1819. It was beautifully restored by the Louisiana Landmarks Society in the 1960s, and is now a museum and a National Trust for Historic Preservation Partner Place. Organized tours are offered in the museum and its sprawling, elegant gardens.

VOODOO ON BAYOU ST. JOHN

Voodoo queen Marie Laveau (see p41) is famous for practicing her rituals on the banks of Bayou St. John. These ceremonies often involved ritualistic dances and animal sacrifices and were witnessed by hundreds of people, believers and skeptics alike.

---

6 Degas House

MAP E2 ▪ 2306 Esplanade Ave ▪ 504-821-5009 ▪ Tours by appt ▪ Adm ▪ www.degashouse.com

Edgar Degas, the renowned French Impressionist painter, lived in this house in 1872–3, and created at least 22 works of art during this period. Today, the house is one of the finest bed-and-breakfast inns in the city. There is an Edgar Degas House Tour, which explores the life of the artist during the Reconstruction Era (the period after the Civil War).

7 The Sydney and Walda Besthoff Sculpture Garden

Named after prominent art patrons collectors, the Besthoffs, this garden includes a collection of contemporary sculpture from across the world. The pieces, donated by the Besthoff Foundation, are displayed among the ancient oaks, magnolias, and tranquil lagoons in this exquisite garden, which is adjacent to the New Orleans Museum of Art. Free mobile guides with information on the sculptures are available (see pp12–15).

8 Angelo Brocato's Ice Cream and Confectionery

MAP C2 ▪ 214 N. Carrollton Ave ▪ 504-486-1465

Angelo Brocato's has managed to retain its quality since opening in 1905. This charming old-world shop, run by the third generation of Brocatos, continues to attract the masses with Italian specialties such as gelato (low-fat ice cream), spumoni (molded Italian ice cream), biscotti (biscuits) and torrone (Italian nougat).

9 New Orleans City Park

Spanning 1,300 acres (526 ha), New Orleans City Park is one of the largest urban parks in the U.S., with a variety of gardens, sculptures, and buildings. Attractions such as Storyland and the Carousel Gardens Amusement Park (see p16) make this a great spot for kids. For visitors interested in outdoor activities, there are golf courses, tennis courts, and waterways for canoeing. The city park also includes the New Orleans Botanical Garden and hosts concerts, festivals, holiday light spectaculars, fundraisers, weddings, and other private events (see pp16–17).

Vintage ride in New Orleans City Park

10 Bayou St. John
MAP J2

One of the most picturesque parts of Mid-City is Bayou St. John, an inner-city creek that separates two residential neighborhoods. Visitors can explore the area on foot or on a bicycle. The bayou is famous for having been the site of voodoo rituals in the 19th century.

Leafy area around Bayou St. John

A TOUR OF NEW ORLEANS CITY PARK

NOLA City Bark 700 yards
Train Garden
Botanical Gardens
Carousel Gardens
Storyland
New Orleans Museum of Art
Sydney and Walda Besthoff Sculpture Garden
Angelo Brocato's 800 yards
Ralph's on the Park

▶ MORNING

Hop on to the Canal streetcar from the French Quarter or downtown area for a scenic ride into Mid-City. The last stop is the **New Orleans Museum of Art** (see pp12–15), where you can get off and explore the museum, as well as walk along handsomely sculptured lawns and flower gardens, under centuries-old oaks, at the **New Orleans City Park** (see pp16–17). This will work up an appetite, so treat yourself to a lavish meal at **Ralph's on the Park** (see p107), which is famous for innovative Creole food as well as its fabulous location.

AFTERNOON

After lunch, walk around the beautifully designed **Sydney and Walda Besthoff Sculpture Garden**. Then make your way to the **New Orleans Botanical Garden** (see p16), where you can view the miniature **Train Garden** (see p17) and also enjoy a walk through the adjacent conservatory and theme gardens. Along the way, be sure to make a stop at **Storyland** (see p16), a delightful place for people of all ages and a special treat for children. From here, walk over to the nearby **Carousel Gardens Amusement Park** (see p16), which houses one of the few remaining antique wooden carousels in the country. Stop by NOLA City Bark, New Orleans' first officially designated dog park. End the day with a delicious *gelato* in one of the many flavors at **Angelo Brocato's Ice Cream and Confectionery**.

See map on p102 ←

Neighborhood Attractions

(1) Mid-City Art Market

MAP B3 ▪ Carrollton Ave ▪ 10am–4pm

On the last Saturday of each month, local artists and craftsmen display and sell their wares at this market in Palmer Park.

(2) American Can Company

MAP H3 ▪ 3700 Orleans Ave ▪ 504-207-0090 ▪ www.americancanapts.com

This condominium complex, a former manufacturing plant, is a prestigious Mid-City address with restaurants and a fashionable shopping area.

(3) Jefferson Davis Monument

MAP C2 ▪ Jefferson Davis Parkway

This controversial stone statue depicts Jefferson Davis, president of the Confederate States during the Civil War. The monument is subject to ongoing legal proceedings that could result in its eventual removal.

(4) Dillard University

2601 Gentilly Blvd ▪ 504-283-8822 ▪ www.dillard.edu

Established in 1869, this liberal-arts college was founded to educate the newly freed African-Americans. It offers majors in six academic fields.

(5) St. Louis Cemetery No. 3

MAP D2 ▪ 3421 Esplanade Ave

A lesser-known cemetery, this is a peaceful place to see New Orleans' peculiar tombs close up. Marble and stone monuments abound.

Mourning angel at St. Louis Cemetery No. 3

A shotgun-style cottage

(6) Shotgun-Style Cottages

These narrow houses found throughout Mid-City have rooms lined up in a single row from front to back. The name derives from the fact that if a shotgun was fired, the bullet would pass straight through the house.

(7) Willie Mae's Scotch House

MAP E2 ▪ 2401 St. Ann St ▪ 504-822-9503 ▪ 11am–3pm Mon–Sat

Said to serve the best fried chicken in New Orleans, Willie Mae's Scotch House has been a very popular eatery since it opened in 1957.

(8) Pandora's Snowballs

MAP H3 ▪ 901 N. Carrollton Ave

A popular local hangout, this small corner shop offers cups of shaved ice in a variety of flavors, creamy soft-serve ice creams, and burgers.

(9) Dueling Oaks

MAP H2 ▪ City Park

In the 19th century, this area in City Park served as a backdrop for countless duels. There's only one large overhanging tree left these days.

(10) The Train Garden

A miniature replica of the city of New Orleans inside the Botanical Garden *(see p16)*, this features a fully operating train and buildings made out of natural materials *(see p17)*.

Places to Eat

 Ralph's on the Park
MAP G2 ■ 900 City Park Ave
■ 504-488-1000 ■ $$$

This stellar restaurant, run by Ralph Brennan, features globally inspired Creole cuisine. The excellent tabasco and honey-glazed flounder is particularly recommended.

 Crescent City Steaks
MAP D2 ■ 1001 N. Broad St
■ 504- 821-3271 ■ Closed Mon ■ $$$

The steaks at this dining room, a favorite since 1934, are outstanding. Curtains wrap around private booths.

Café Minh
MAP C2 ■ 4139 Canal St
■ 504-482-6266 ■ Closed Sun ■ $$

Renowned for its French-Vietnamese fusion cuisine, Café Minh's specials include coconut shrimp, crab cakes, and crabmeat and sweet corn soup.

Parkway Bakery and Tavern
MAP D2 ■ 538 Hagan Ave ■ 866-755-9842 ■ $$ ■ Closed Tue

This quaint shop serves some of the best fried shrimp po'boys (see p57) and roast beef sandwiches in the city.

Lola's
MAP D2 ■ 3312 Esplanade Ave
■ 504-488-6946 ■ $$$

This popular Spanish restaurant allows patrons to bring their own wine. Try the seafood paella.

Venezia
MAP C2 ■ 134 North Carrollton Ave ■ 504-488-7991 ■ Closed Mon–Tue ■ $$

Thanks to its authentic Italian dishes, Venezia is a popular local haunt. The pizzas are excellent.

Mandina's Restaurant
MAP C2 ■ 3800 Canal St ■ 504-482-9179 ■ $$

A local institution, Mandina's serves delicacies such as jambalaya and a hearty gumbo (see p56).

PRICE CATEGORIES
For a three-course meal for one, with half a bottle of wine (or equivalent meal), taxes, and extra charges.
....
$ under $25 $$ $25–$50 $$$ over $50

Dooky Chase
MAP E3 ■ 2301 Orleans Ave ■ 504-821-0600 ■ Closed Sat–Mon ■ $$

Run by legendary chef Leah Chase, who is famous for her authentic "Creole Soul" food, Dooky Chase has delicious home cooking.

Café Degas
MAP D2 ■ 3127 Esplanade Ave ■ 504-945-5635 ■ Closed Mon–Tue ■ $$

Named for the Impressionist artist Edgar Degas, this diminutive picturesque French bistro excels in light, subtle dishes.

Charming ambience at Café Degas

 Liuzza's
MAP C2 ■ 3636 Bienville St
■ 504-482-9120 ■ Closed Mon
■ $$

Famous for its meatballs, seafood lasagna, jambalaya, and huge, icy "fishbowls" of draft beer, Liuzza's is a busy but friendly neighborhood diner.

See map on p102 ←

Streetsmart

**Bright-red streetcars, commonly
seen on the streets of New Orleans**

Getting To and Around New Orleans

Arriving by Air

Most major U.S. airlines offer domestic and international flights to New Orleans. Located about 15 miles (24 km) from downtown New Orleans, the **Louis Armstrong International Airport** is modern and efficient. The luggage-claim areas and exits to ground transport services are downstairs.

Public transport options from the airport include the no. 202 Airport Express run by **RTA** (Regional Transport Authority), with nine daily trips priced at $1.50; an affordable shared shuttle bus operated by **Airport Shuttle New Orleans**, serving downtown hotels; and cabs, which you can find at the stand outside the arrivals hall. A typical trip to downtown costs in the region of $35–40.

Arriving by Rail

Three major **Amtrak** trains serve the city: City of New Orleans, from Chicago; Crescent, from New York's Penn Station; and Sunset Limited, from Orlando and Los Angeles. All make stops at major cities. The **New Orleans Union Passenger Terminal** is located at the edge of the Central Business District.

Arriving by Road

Greyhound buses serve New Orleans from around 4,000 U.S. locations. The city's **Greyhound Bus Station** is well located on the edge of the Central Business District, close to most downtown hotels.

Driving to the city gives you some independence; however, parking can be a challenge, especially downtown. The main Interstate Highway that serves New Orleans is the I-10.

Arriving by Sea

Over a million passengers arrive in New Orleans via cruise lines, such as **Carnival** and **Norwegian**. The **Port of New Orleans** is in the Central Business District, not far from the Convention Center.

Traveling by Bus and Streetcar

Run by the RTA, the bus system has been enhanced over the past few years with more frequent and reliable services, improved routes and new lines to increase access to all parts of the city.

Streetcars (also run by RTA) are great for getting around New Orleans, and a good way to really see the city. They aren't just a tourist attraction – locals use them to travel around the city all the time. Streetcars move at a moderate pace and stop frequently, allowing passengers to see the sights and even take photographs along the way. They are also a pleasant, breezy way to travel in the hottest days of summer.

The standard fare for a single journey on the bus or streetcar is $1.25. Transfers cost 25 cents each. Children under 2 years of age ride free. An RTA Jazzy Pass, available in 1-, 3-, and 31-day versions, lets you ride both buses and streetcars.

Traveling by Taxi

There are taxi stands outside some of the city's bigger hotels, and you can also flag one down on the street. The largest taxi company is **United Cabs**. Ordering by telephone will usually get a cab to you within a few minutes. Taxis are inexpensive and take credit cards.

Traveling by Car

Apart from expensive parking lots, there are few places to park in the city. Avoid driving through the French Quarter, with its antiquated streets and carriage-ride circuits. Some hotels allow guests to park their cars for a $20–40 daily fee. Downtown New Orleans is compact, and visitors usually find it more convenient to take public transport.

Traveling by Bicycle

The flat landscape of New Orleans is favorable for cyclists, and the number of cycle lanes is constantly rising. In 2015, the Lafitte Greenway opened, connecting Armstrong and City Parks with a 2.6-mile (4.2-km) bicycle trail. Some of the streets are in a state of disrepair, though, and heavy downtown traffic makes it imperative to follow safety precautions. Observe stoplights and stop signs and stay as close to the curb as possible. Cycling at night is not advisable. You can hire bikes from companies such as **A Bicycle Named Desire** or **Confederacy of Cruisers**.

Traveling by Steamboat and Ferry

Paddlewheel steamboats still circuit the Mississippi River around New Orleans. A great way to spend the evening is to take a dinner cruise, or spend an afternoon on a riverboat tour learning about the city's history. You can book at the **New Orleans Steamboat Company**, which has a booth on the riverfront.

A **New Orleans Ferry** service runs from the Central Business District to New Orleans' West Bank neighborhood. The Chalmette ferry accommodates cars, while the Algiers service is only for foot passengers. The journey takes only a few minutes and affords great views looking back over the New Orleans skyline.

Traveling by Carriage

An enjoyable way to see the French Quarter and some of the surrounding neighborhoods is by horse-drawn carriage. These can be hired privately, by a couple or family, or shared with other small groups. The carriages are around Decatur Street near Jackson Square. Drivers are trained tour guides and will regale you with historical anecdotes as you trot around the city.

Traveling on Foot

New Orleans is a great city to explore on foot. Walking allows you to take in the architecture and the details of the historic buildings. The downtown areas are close enough to walk between, and from the CBD all the way to the Bywater is only a couple of miles' walk through pleasant surroundings. Take care walking around at night, though. Stick to the busiest streets and avoid poorly lit areas.

DIRECTORY

ARRIVING BY AIR

Airport Shuttle New Orleans
🌐 airportshuttle-neworleans.com

Louis Armstrong International Airport
MAP B2
🌐 flymsy.com

RTA
🌐 norta.com

ARRIVING BY RAIL

Amtrak
🌐 amtrak.com

New Orleans Union Passenger Terminal
MAP P1 ■ 1001 Loyola Ave
Open 5am–10pm daily
🌐 amtrak.com

ARRIVING BY ROAD

Greyhound Bus Station
MAP P1
■ 1001 Loyola Ave
📞 504-525-6075
Open 5:15am–9:25pm daily (closed 10:30–11:30am & 1–2:30pm)
🌐 greyhound.com

ARRIVING BY SEA

Carnival Cruise Line
🌐 carnival.com

Norwegian Cruise Line
🌐 ncl.com

Port of New Orleans
1350 Port of New Orleans Place
📞 504-522-2551
🌐 portno.com

TRAVELING BY TAXI

United Cabs
📞 504-522-9771
🌐 unitedcabs.com

TRAVELING BY BICYCLE

A Bicycle Named Desire
MAP K6 ■ 632 Elysian Fields Ave
📞 504-345-8966
🌐 abicyclenameddesire.com

Confederacy of Cruisers
MAP K6 ■ 634 Elysian Fields Ave
📞 504-400-5468
🌐 confederacyofcruisers.com

TRAVELING BY STEAMBOAT AND FERRY

New Orleans Ferry
Landing points: 1 Canal St; 101 Morgan St, Algiers Point; 7360 Patterson Dr, Lower Algiers; 1600 Paris Rd, Chalmette
📞 504-309-9789
🌐 nolaferries.com

New Orleans Steamboat Company
MAP M5 ■ Steamboat Natchez Lighthouse Ticket Office: Toulouse St at the riverfront
📞 800-233-2628, 504-569-1401
🌐 neworleanssteamboatcompany.com

Practical Information

Passports and Visas

Citizens from Visa Waiver Program (VWP) countries can travel to New Orleans without a visa if they meet certain requirements. However, they must file an online Electronic System for Travel Authorization (ESTA) form at the **U.S. Customs and Border Protection** website well in advance of their trip, and produce a valid passport at the port of entry. Canadian citizens require only proof of residence.

The nearest consulates of the **U.K.**, **Australia**, and **Canada** are in Texas, while the **New Zealand** consulate is in New York.

Customs Regulations

Visitors over the age of 21 traveling from abroad have the right to carry up to 200 cigarettes, 1.75 pints (1 liter) of alcohol, and 4.4 lb (2 kg) of pipe tobacco. Plants, fresh foods such as cheese, and meat are prohibited, as, of course, are weapons and non-prescription drugs.

Travel Safety Advice

Up-to-date travel safety information is available from the **U.S. Department of State**, **Australian Department of Foreign Affairs and Trade**, and **U.K. Foreign and Commonwealth Office**. For more information, check the National Terrorism Advisory System on the website of the **U.S. Department of Homeland Security**.

Travel Insurance

Due to the high cost of local healthcare, it is extremely unwise to travel to the U.S. without first buying valid insurance.

Health

For urgent medical care, go to the emergency rooms at **Touro Infirmary** or the **University Medical Center New Orleans** (UMCNO). For dental emergencies, call UMCNO or the **New Orleans Dental Association**; both are open 24 hours daily.

If you take medication, it is wise to bring a back-up prescription with you. The city has several **RiteAid** and **Walgreens** pharmacies. Those close to the French Quarter are open 9am–7pm daily. There are also several 24-hour pharmacies; ask your hotel for assistance.

Personal Security

The streets of New Orleans are generally safe as long as you exercise good judgment. If possible, stay in a large group when sightseeing outside, and do not challenge a thief. Do not advertise the fact that you are a visitor (e.g. do not wear Mardi Gras beads outside of Mardi Gras season), and prepare the day's itinerary in advance. Avoid wearing flashy jewelry, and carry your phone securely. Only carry small amounts of cash; credit cards are more secure options. Most crime is contained within residential areas, and it is unlikely that a visitor would wander into these neighborhoods.

Emergency Services

To contact the authorities for fire, police, or an ambulance, dial the **emergencies** number 911 free of charge from any phone. For non-emergency situations, call the **non-emergencies** number.

Natural Hazards

Hurricanes are infrequent but devastating when they do strike. If there is a storm, follow the announcements on local television and radio. A hotline may be set up before a storm. If an evacuation order is given, leave the area immediately. Ignoring this order or waiting until the last minute could prove disastrous. The **National Hurricane Center** has online forecasts.

Disabled Travelers

There are elevators, ramps, and special parking spaces all around the city. Historic properties are exempt from accessibility laws, however, so not many have most these facilities, nor do most restaurants and bars. Call ahead to confirm. Outside of the French Quarter and downtown, sidewalks may not be suitable for wheelchairs. The Canal and Riverfront streetcar routes and all RTA buses have wheelchair ramps. For more information, call the **Advocacy Center**.

Trips and Tours

A range of city tours led by licensed guides is available. Walking tours cover themes such as jazz, history, architecture, and cemeteries; try the **French Quarter Phantoms** ghost tours (see p46).

Confederacy of Cruisers (see p111) runs bicycle tours. Segway tours, such as those run by **City Segway Tours**, are also popular. Narrated bus tours service all areas outside the French Quarter. **City Sightseeing** runs an excellent hop-on, hop-off bus tour.

Bayou and wetlands tours by swamp-boat operators such as **Jean Lafitte Swamp Tours** are an exciting way to experience the local wildlife (see p48). Transport to the boat launch is usually provided.

Visitor Information

The **NOCVB** (New Orleans Convention and Visitors Bureau) and the **New Orleans Tourism Marketing Corporation** are useful sources of information. The NOCVB offers free maps, as well as discount coupons for certain establishments. It can also assist in cases of loss or theft of personal items, and accidents.

DIRECTORY

PASSPORTS AND VISAS

Australian Consulate, Houston
832-962-8420
usa.embassy.gov.au

Canadian Consulate, Dallas
214-922-9806
can-am.gc.ca/dallas

New Zealand Consulate, New York
212-832-4038
nzembassy.com/united-states-of-america

U.K. Consulate, Houston
713-210-4000
ukinusa.fco.gov.uk

U.S. Customs and Border Protection
esta.cbp.dhs.gov/esta

TRAVEL SAFETY ADVICE

Australian Department of Foreign Affairs and Trade
dfat.gov.au
smartraveller.gov.au

U.K. Foreign and Commonwealth Office
gov.uk/foreign-travel-advice

U.S. Department of Homeland Security
dhs.gov/national-terrorism-advisory-system

U.S. Department of State
travel.state.gov

HEALTH

New Orleans Dental Association
504-834-6449
nodental.org

RiteAid
MAP L1 ■ 2669 Canal St
504-827-1400
riteaid.com

Touro Infirmary
MAP G6
■ 1401 Foucher St
504-897-7011
touro.com

University Medical Center New Orleans
MAP L1 ■ 2000 Canal St
504-702-3000, 504 702-2138
umcno.org

Walgreens
MAP S1 ■ 1801 St Charles Ave
504-561-8458
walgreens.com

EMERGENCY SERVICES

Emergencies
911

Non-emergencies
504-821-2222

NATURAL HAZARDS

National Hurricane Center
nhc.noaa.gov

DISABLED TRAVELERS

Advocacy Center
MAP A4 ■ 8325 Oak St
800-960-7705

TRIPS AND TOURS

City Segway Tours
504-619-4162
citysegwaytours.com

City Sightseeing
MAP N4 ■ 700 Decatur St & 501 Basin St
800-362-1811
citysightseeing neworleans.com

VISITOR INFORMATION

NOCVB
MAP J4 ■ 2020 St Charles Ave
800-672-6124
neworleanscvb.com

New Orleans Tourism Marketing Corporation
MAP N4 ■ 365 Canal St
504-524-4784
neworleansonline.com

Currency and Banking

Banks are generally open 9am–4pm Monday to Friday. Some, however, open as early as 8:30am and stay open until 5pm. Most New Orleans banks have ATMs outside or in their lobbies. ATMs can also be found in bars and restaurants, especially in the French Quarter. Many charge a fee.

Telephone and Internet

Finding Wi-Fi hotspots is usually easy – most hotel lobbies, cafés, and coffee shops offer customers free Internet access. Most high-end hotels charge daily fees for Internet access in guest rooms. Public telephones are increasingly rare and frequently out of service. **FedEx Kinko's** and the **French Quarter Postal Emporium** offer printing and shipping services.

Postal Services

Post offices are usually open 9am–5pm Monday to Friday, with some branches also open on Saturday mornings. Drugstores and hotels sell stamps. The **Main Post Office** is downtown, while couriers such as **UPS**, **DHL**, and **FedEx** offer next-day deliveries to most destinations.

TV, Radio, and Newspapers

The local daily newspaper is **The Times-Picayune.** The free weekly paper **Gambit** is a good source of entertainment news.

Several local monthly magazines, such as **Offbeat** and **Where Y'at Magazine,** offer local news, plus restaurant, nightlife, festival, and event listings.

Most hotels have national TV, plus either cable or satellite. National Public Radio WWNO (89.9 FM) focuses on national news and classical music; the Jazz and Heritage Foundation station WWOZ (90.7 FM) has R&B, jazz, and zydeco.

Opening Hours

Museums tend to open 10am–5pm. Most stores are open 10am–6pm, but souvenir stores in the French Quarter close later. Restaurants usually start evening service at 5pm and continue until 10pm (11pm Friday and Saturday), or until the last diner leaves. Live music usually starts at 10pm, and it is a tradition not to close until the last guest has left. Many places (attractions and restaurants) are closed on Mondays.

Time Difference

New Orleans is six hours behind Greenwich Mean Time, 17 hours behind Australia, and 19 hours behind New Zealand.

Electrical Appliances

Electrical current flows at 110 volts AC, and appliances require two-prong plugs. Some non-US appliances will require both a plug converter and a 110–120 volt adaptor compatible with the U.S. electricity system.

Weather

With their temperate weather, spring and fall are the best times to visit. From May through September, the weather is hot and humid, but the city is still busy with both indoor and outdoor events. From October through March, the temperature is colder, and there are often heavy fogs. New Orleans is one of the rainiest cities in the U.S., and July and August have daily showers. The hurricane season lasts from June to November, peaking in August and September.

Smoking and Alcohol

Smoking is prohibited in all public buildings, including stores and restaurants. The legal age for drinking alcohol is 21; however, anybody may be asked for photo ID to get into bars. If you wish to consume an alcoholic drink on the street, it must be in a plastic container, or "go cup."

Shopping

Stores in the CBD, along Magazine Street, and in the French Quarter tend to operate 9am–5pm or 10am–6pm. Some shops in the Quarter don't open until noon, but they also close late. Many open on Sundays, but call in advance to check. Local shops are often closed on Mondays.

If you are a foreign visitor, you can get back the 10 per cent sales tax on tangible goods, but you must show the vendor your passport and ask for a refund voucher. At the airport, go to the **Louisiana Tax Free Shopping Refund Center** with your passport, sales receipts, refund vouchers, and air ticket (which may be for up to a maximum of a 90-day trip). If you are not reimbursed at the airport, send copies of everything, along with an explanation, to the Refund Center.

Where to Eat

Food is a religion in this city. There are more than 1,000 restaurants in the greater New Orleans area, many of them rooted in the Louisiana Creole tradition. Cajun and Creole cuisines are somewhat intertwined, both utilizing the plentiful seafood and spices of the region. However, the culinary landscape is becoming more diverse, with Italian, Vietnamese, and other ethnic eateries. High-end restaurants are found throughout the city, particularly in the Uptown and Downtown neighbor-hoods, with many acclaimed establishments to be found in the Marigny and the Bywater districts.

The city also has many excellent coffee shops offering baked items. Several hotels have good dining rooms open to the public, and various delis and corner groceries sell sandwiches or pre-prepared meals known as "hot lunch." There are also plenty of places for inexpensive food, such as po'boys, muffuletta (both local variations on the sandwich), pizza, and the ubiquitous dish of red beans and rice with sausage. Look out for mobile food trucks and "pop-up" eateries.

New Orleans' restaurant prices offer relatively good value, and are notably lower than their New York or San Francisco counterparts.

Where to Stay

The vast majority of New Orleans hotels are in the French Quarter and the CBD. Prices depend on the location and the level of luxury. They can rise by more than 100 per cent during Mardi Gras, Jazz Fest, holidays, and other events. Booking at least six months in advance is recommended for Mardi Gras, and a minimum stay is often required. Boutique hotels and guesthouses are usually in attractive renovated historic homes. Most offer some meals, full breakfasts or coffee and pastries; often, afternoon tea or cocktails are also provided. Larger hotels may have one or two fine restaurants, several bars, a fitness room, a swimming pool, spa, and a business center. At virtually every hotel, you will find complimentary toiletries, newspapers, room service, and wake-up and reservation services. All accommodations are air conditioned. B&Bs generally do not offer all these amenities, often due to the historic character of the building (renovations and improvements are very strictly regulated).

All hotels in the U.S. are required by law to provide wheelchair-accessible accommodations, but designated historic properties are exempt from this provision.

DIRECTORY

TELEPHONE AND INTERNET

FedEx Kinko's
MAP P3
■ 762 St. Charles Ave
(504-581-2541
w fedex.com/us/office

French Quarter Postal Emporium
MAP L4
■ 1000 Bourbon St
(504-525-6651
w frenchquarterpostal. net

POSTAL SERVICES

Main Post Office
MAP P2
■ 701 Loyola Ave
(800-275-8777
w usps.com

DHL
(800-225-5345
w dhl.com

FedEx
(800-463-3339
w fedex.com

UPS
(800-742-5877
w ups.com

TV, RADIO, AND NEWSPAPERS

Gambit
w bestofneworleans.com

Offbeat
w offbeat.com

The Times-Picayune
w nola.com

Where Y'at Magazine
w whereyat.com

SHOPPING

Louisiana Tax Free Shopping Refund Center
(504-467-0723
w louisianataxfree.com

Places to Stay

PRICE CATEGORIES

For a standard double room per night during high season, including taxes and service charges.

$ under $100 $$ $100–250 $$$ over $250

Luxury Hotels

AC Hotel New Orleans Bourbon
MAP N3 ■ 221 Carondelet St ■ 504-962-0700 ■ www.mariott.com/msyac ■ $$$
This stylish hotel is housed in a former 19th-century cotton trade center. Craft cocktails are served in the lounge.

Ace Hotel New Orleans
MAP P3 ■ 600 Carondelet St ■ 504-900-1180 ■ www.acehotel.com ■ $$$
The hip Ace Hotel chain debuted in the city in 2016 in this renovated historic 1928 Art Deco building. A rooftop garden, poolside dining, 234 stylish rooms, and on-site music venue, Three Keys, make this a chic choice.

Hotel Monteleone
MAP M3 ■ 214 Royal St ■ 504-523-3341 ■ www.hotelmonteleone.com ■ $$$
The grande dame of New Orleans luxury hotels, the Monteleone is said to be haunted, but that has not affected its popularity. It has sublime rooms, a spa, and restaurants (see p29).

International House Hotel
MAP N3 ■ 221 Camp St ■ 504-553-9550 ■ www.ihhotel.com ■ $$$
The lobby at this hotel with beautifully appointed rooms is "dressed" for summer and winter, an old New Orleans ritual. Have a drink at Loa, the hip hotel lounge (see p82).

Old No. 77 Hotel & Chandlery
MAP P4 ■ 535 Tchoupitoulas St ■ 504-527-5271 ■ www.old77hotel.com ■ $$$
The former Ambassador Hotel has been sensitively renovated into one of the city's most exciting hotels. Rooms feature hardwood floors, exposed brick, and local art, plus locally distilled rum in the mini-bar.

The Ritz-Carlton, New Orleans
MAP M3 ■ 921 Canal St ■ 504-561-0500 ■ www.ritzcarlton.com ■ $$$
This hotel located in an artfully renovated historic building, formerly a department store, has some of the finest rooms in the city, and the service is impeccable (see p36).

The Roosevelt New Orleans
MAP N3 ■ 130 Roosevelt Way ■ 504-648-1200 ■ www.therooseveltneworleans.com ■ $$$
Gold-leaf columns decorate the lobby of this historic hotel, now part of Waldorf Astoria. The Roosevelt's legendary Blue Room, where the likes of Louis Armstrong and Ray Charles used to perform, is hired out for events (see p37).

W New Orleans – French Quarter
MAP M4 ■ 316 Chartres St ■ 504-581-1200 ■ www.wfrenchquarter.com ■ $$$
This boutique-style W has tastefully decorated rooms, an award-winning restaurant, a courtyard and a heated outdoor pool.

Westin Canal Place
MAP N4 ■ 100 Iberville St ■ 504-566-7006 ■ www.westin.com ■ $$$
This hotel overlooking the Mississippi spells sheer grandeur, with an elegant dining room, a beautiful lobby with large French windows, and spacious, well-appointed rooms.

Windsor Court Hotel
MAP N4 ■ 300 Gravier St ■ 504-523-6000 ■ www.windsorcourthotel.com ■ $$$
Arguably the city's finest contemporary hotel, this boasts an excellent art collection, plush rooms, and a fine-dining spot, The Grill Room.

Vintage Hotels

Cornstalk Hotel
MAP L5 ■ 915 Royal St ■ 504-523-1515 ■ www.cornstalkhotel.com ■ $$
Famous for its cornstalk-shaped cast-iron fence, this charming, intimate hotel occupies a converted 19th-century home (see p28).

Inn on St. Peter
MAP L4 ■ 1005 St. Peter St ■ 800-535-7815 ■ www.frenchquarterguesthouses.com ■ $$
In the French Quarter, Inn on St. Peter has central

courtyards and iron-lace balconies that lend it a flavor of the Old South.

Lafayette Hotel
MAP P3 ▪ 600 St. Charles Ave ▪ 1-888-626-5457 ▪ www.thelafayettehotel.com ▪ $$
Dating back to 1916, this hotel has been restored to its original splendor. Its period decor is complemented by French doors and wrought-iron balconies. The St. Charles streetcar stops just outside.

Lamothe House Hotel
MAP K5 ▪ 621 Esplanade Ave ▪ 800-367-5858 ▪ www.frenchquarterguesthouses.com ▪ $$
This hotel provides a truly vintage New Orleans experience in a 19th-century mansion.

Le Pavillon Hotel
MAP P2 ▪ 833 Poydras St ▪ 504-581-3111 ▪ www.lepavillon.com ▪ $$
Boasting a majestic lobby with high ceilings, chandeliers, and a grand dining room, and a hotel has a distinct old-world charm.

Pontchartrain Hotel
MAP S1 ▪ 2031 St. Charles Ave ▪ 504-206-3114 ▪ www.thepontchartrainhotel.com ▪ $$
The new incarnation of this hotel, which first opened in 1912, mixes old-world rooms with revamped public spaces, including a hip rooftop bar.

Prince Conti Hotel
MAP M3 ▪ 830 Conti St ▪ 800-366-2743 ▪ www.princecontihotel.com ▪ $$
The ambience here is that of a 19th-century French chateau. Rooms are

elegant, and the service is superb. The stylish Bombay Club serves Creole food.

St. James Hotel
MAP P4 ▪ 330 Magazine St ▪ 504-304-4000 ▪ www.saintjameshotel.com ▪ $$
Housed in a 19th-century former trading center, the St. James has West Indian decor reflecting its Caribbean sugar and coffee trade past.

Omni Royal Orleans
MAP M4 ▪ 621 St. Louis St ▪ 504-529-5333 ▪ www.omnihotels.com ▪ $$$
This elegant, beautifully maintained French Quarter hotel houses the fine gourmet restaurant, Rib Room (see p29).

Royal Sonesta Hotel
MAP M4 ▪ 300 Bourbon St ▪ 504-586-0300 ▪ www.royalsonesta.com ▪ $$$
The elegant Royal Sonesta combines a rich heritage with modern amenities. It is home to The Jazz Playhouse (see p33).

Soniat House
MAP L5 ▪ 133 Chartres St ▪ 504-522-0570 ▪ www.soniathouse.com ▪ $$$
Built in 1829, Soniat House has the intimacy of a private home. Rooms are individually decorated with attention to details. The hotel is a favorite with celebrities.

Business Hotels

Hilton Garden Inn – New Orleans Convention Center
MAP R4 ▪ 1001 South Peters St ▪ 504-525-0044 ▪ www.hiltongardeninn3.hilton.com ▪ $$
Just across from the Morial Convention Center,

this modern property has a relaxed ambience and an American restaurant.

Hilton Riverside Hotel
MAP P4 ▪ 2 Poydras St ▪ 504-561-0500 ▪ www.hilton.com ▪ $$
Located on the banks of the Mississippi, this large hotel is a favorite with business travelers heading to the nearby Ernest N. Morial Convention Center.

Hyatt French Quarter
MAP L2 ▪ 800 Iberville St ▪ 504-586-0800 ▪ www.frenchquarter.hyatt.com ▪ $$
Spacious rooms have clean design touches and high ceilings. Guests can enjoy the outdoor pool area and cocktails at the hotel bar.

Le Méridien New Orleans
MAP P2 ▪ 333 Poydras St ▪ 504-525-9444 ▪ www.lemeridienneworleanshotel.com ▪ $$
This former W hotel has been redesigned with an emphasis on contemporary decor influenced by New Orleans culture.

Harrah's New Orleans Hotel
MAP P4 ▪ 228 Poydras St ▪ 504-523-6000 ▪ www.harrahsneworleans.com ▪ $$$
On a busy crossing in the downtown area, Harrah's offers state-of-the-art, spacious rooms (see p36).

Hotel Inter-Continental
MAP N3 ▪ 444 St. Charles Ave ▪ 504-525-5566 ▪ www.ichotelsgroup.com ▪ $$$
Large rooms with modern workspace accessories make this hotel popular with business travelers.

Hyatt Regency New Orleans

MAP P2 ▪ 601 Loyola Ave ▪ 504-561-1234 ▪ www.neworleans. hyatt.com ▪ $$$

This vast hotel overlooking the Mercedes-Benz Superdome [see p80] has an extensive meeting and exhibition space.

Loews Hotel

MAP P4 ▪ 300 Poydras St ▪ 504-595-3300 ▪ www. loewshotels.com ▪ $$$

No expense has been spared on the furnishings, lighting, and art adorning this hotel, which features some of the largest rooms in the city.

Renaissance Pere Marquette

MAP N3 ▪ 817 Common St ▪ 504-525-1111 ▪ www.marriott.com ▪ $$$

This historic downtown hotel has been renovated into a luxurious property with stylish decor.

Sheraton New Orleans Hotel

MAP N4 ▪ 500 Canal St ▪ 504-525-2500 ▪ www. sheratonneworleans.com ▪ $$$

Spacious rooms, modern amenities, and a central location ensure a loyal clientele. There are five majestic ballrooms and 54 meeting rooms.

Mid-Range Hotels

Aloft New Orleans Downtown

MAP N3 ▪ 225 Baronne St ▪ 504-581-9225 ▪ www. aloftneworleansdown town.com ▪ $$

The 188 loft-style rooms are minimalist but chic, with plush bedding and upscale amenities. The fitness center, outdoor pool, and neon-lit W XYZ lobby bar make this hotel great value.

Avenue Plaza Resort

MAP J4 ▪ 2111 St. Charles Ave ▪ 504-566-1212 ▪ www.avenueplazaresort. com ▪ $$

This all-suite hotel bills itself as a resort with a swimming pool. All the rooms reflect an old-world charm and have their own kitchenettes.

Blake Hotel

MAP P3 ▪ 500 St. Charles Ave ▪ 504-522-9000 ▪ www.blakehotelnew orleans.com ▪ $$

The finely renovated Blake Hotel is a short walk from the riverfront and the St. Charles streetcar.

Bon Maison Guest House

MAP L4 ▪ 835 Bourbon St ▪ 504-561-8498 ▪ www. bonmaison.com ▪ $$

This 19th-century town house close to the French Quarter has been refashioned into a guesthouse built around a beautiful courtyard.

Catahoula Hotel

MAP N2 ▪ 914 Union St ▪ 504-603-2442 ▪ www. catahoulahotel.com ▪ $$

Set in a charmingly restored Creole town house, this chic, modern hotel has a lovely rooftop terrace, Peruvian café, and Pisco Bar.

Columns Hotel

MAP C6 ▪ 3811 St. Charles Ave ▪ 504-899-9308 ▪ www.thecolumns. com ▪ $$

Relaxing with a cocktail on the Columns' front porch is an ideal way to start your holiday at this Italianate building designed in 1883 by New Orleans architect, Thomas Sully. The rooms are a little old-fashioned, but the moderate pricing makes it worthwhile.

Dauphine Orleans Hotel

MAP M3 ▪ 415 Dauphine St ▪ 504-586-1800 ▪ www.dauphineorleans. com ▪ $$

This French Quarter hotel includes a number of 19th-century buildings that were inhabited by the artist John James Audubon. Rooms are modern, and there's complimentary breakfast and Wi-Fi, plus an outdoor saltwater pool.

Hotel Le Marais

MAP M3 ▪ 717 Conti St ▪ 504-525-2300 ▪ www. hotellemarais.com ▪ $$

A modern addition to a historic district, Le Marais is half a block from Bourbon Street, right in the thick of the action. The courtyard offers a welcome respite, and the heated saltwater pool is lovely. The interior design is striking, with bold, chic colors and there is also a good complimentary continental breakfast.

Hotel Mazarin

MAP M3 ▪ 730 Bienville St ▪ 504-581-7300 ▪ www.hotelmazarin.com ▪ $$

Rooms at this hotel set back from the bustle of Bourbon Street boast black granite bathrooms and high-end cotton bedding. The attached wine bar is a nice amenity, and the complimentary breakfast is wonderful.

Moxy New Orleans Downtown
MAP N2 ■ 210 O'Keefe Ave ■ 504-525-6800 ■ www.moxynola.com ■ $$
This spirited, vibrant boutique hotel is near the French Quarter. Modern touches include 24/7 self-service nibbles, a popular cocktail bar, and free high-speed Internet.

The Whitney Hotel
MAP N1 ■ 610 Poydras Str ■ 504-581-4222 ■ www.whitneyhotel.com ■ $$
The architecture of this hotel, in a former bank in the CBD, gives it a novel feel. The original vault is a notable feature, as are the brass fittings and crown moldings. The traditionally decorated rooms are extremely quiet thanks to the property's thick walls.

Best Western Plus St. Charles Inn
MAP C6 ■ 3636 St. Charles Ave ■ 504-899-8888 ■ www.bestwestern louisiana.com ■ $$$
The St. Charles Inn is in a busy part of town dotted with good restaurants. The streetcar stops right outside, providing access to most city attractions.

Bed and Breakfast

Ashton's Bed & Breakfast
MAP E2 ■ 2023 Esplanade Ave ■ 504-942-7048 ■ www.ashtonsbb.com ■ $$
This Greek Revival mansion has been lovingly transformed into a bed and breakfast. The main house features high ceilings, spacious rooms, and some fine period furnishings.

Avenue Inn
MAP C6 ■ 4125 St. Charles Ave ■ 504-269-2640 ■ www.avenueinn bb.com ■ $$
Guests can choose from a range of rooms at this beautiful house located among ancient oak trees on the streetcar line.

Chimes Bed & Breakfast
MAP C6 ■ 1146 Constantinople St ■ 504-899-2621 ■ www.chimes neworleans.com ■ $$
This uptown inn oozes historic charm. Each of the five rooms has French doors opening onto a common courtyard. The rooms have their own private entrance.

Claiborne Mansion
MAP K6 ■ 2111 Dauphine St ■ 504-949-7327 ■ www.claibornemansion. com ■ $$
Located in the Faubourg Marigny, this is one of the most elegantly restored mansions in the area. It is designed to make guests feel like they are staying in a private home.

Dauphine House
MAP K5 ■ 1830 Dauphine St ■ 504-940-0943 ■ www. dauphinehouse.com ■ $$
Built in 1860, Dauphine House has high ceilings and hardwood floors, and is just around the corner from the French Quarter. For most months of the year some rooms are available for under $100.

Degas House
MAP E2 ■ 2306 Esplanade Ave ■ 504-821-5009 ■ www.degashouse.com ■ $$
French Impressionist Edgar Degas stayed and

painted in this house on a picturesque street.It is now a well-maintained bed and breakfast (see p104).

Lafitte Guest House
MAP L4 ■ 1003 Bourbon St ■ 504-581-2678 ■ www.lafitteguesthouse. com ■ $$
A restored mid-19th-century property in the heart of the French Quarter, this guesthouse is richly decorated and has rooms filled with antiques and a quiet courtyard.

Melrose Mansion
MAP K5 ■ 937 Esplanade Ave ■ MAP K5 ■ 504-944-2255 ■ www.melrose mansion.com ■ $$
Set in a huge Victorian Gothic-style mansion built in 1884, this luxurious bed-and-breakfast is imbued with old-world charm. It features one of the most romantic suites in the city.

Sully Mansion
MAP H5 ■ 631 Prytania St ■ 504-891-0457 ■ www. sullymansion.com ■ $$
Designed in 1890 by local architect Thomas Sully, this mansion has a lovely wraparound porch. It has just nine guest rooms and is quite close to the St. Charles streetcar line.

The Henry Howard Hotel
MAP J4 ■ 2041 Prytania St ■ 504-313-1577 ■ www. henryhoward hotel.com ■ $$$
Named for the man who built this mansion in 1867, this hotel is an elegant blend of traditional vintage furniture and modern amenities. The Parlor is a splendid setting to sip a craft cocktail.

For a key to hotel price categories see p116

General Index

Acknowledgments

Author
Paul Greenberg is a journalist and professor who lives in New Orleans. He decided to made the city her permanent home because of its rich culture, history, and outstanding food. He has written for regional and local publications and has authored several local travel guidebooks.

Additional contributor
Paul Oswell

Publishing Director Georgina Dee

Publisher Vivien Antwi

Design Director Phil Ormerod

Editorial Ankita Awasthi Tröger, Michelle Crane, Rachel Fox, Maresa Manara, Rada Radojicic, Akshay Rana, Sally Schafer, Sands Publishing Solutions, Akanksha Siwach

Design Hansa Babra, Tessa Bindloss, Sunita Gahir, Rahul Kumar

Cover Design Richard Czapnik

Commissioned Photography Rough Guides / Greg Ward 27bl, 30cb, 106bl; Helena Smith 7tr, 30tl, 55clb, 60tc, 61tc,104tl; Stuart West 57br.

Picture Research Susie Peachey, Ellen Root, Lucy Sienkowska, Oran Tarjan

Cartography Zafar ul Islam Khan, Suresh Kumar, Casper Morris, Reetu Pandey

DTP Jason Little

Production Olivia Jeffries

Factchecker Ella Buchan

Proofreader Clare Peele

Indexer Hilary Bird

Picture Credits
The publisher would like to thank the following for their kind permission to reproduce their photographs:

Key: a-above; b-below/bottom; c-centre; f-far; l-left; r-right; t-top

123RF.com: legacy1995 92bl.

Alamy Stock Photo: Irene Abdou 16-7, 17bl, 81bl; Rolf Adlercreutz 27c; age fotostock / Judie Long 45cl; Charles O. Cecil 36cla, 37tl, 82tl, 88cl, 100t; Ian Dagnall 60b, 73crb, 91tl; Danita Delimont / Jamie & Judy Wild 10cl; GJGK Photography 44t; Tim Graham 69tr, 93tl; Granger Historical Picture Archive 41cla; Spencer Grant 46crb, 65cl, 96cl; hemis.fr / Gil Giuglio 11cra, / Patrick Frilet 11bl; Gerrit De Heus 47tr; Robert Holmes 2tr, 38-9; Peter Horree 11cl; James Houser New Orleans 98-9, 104-5; Images-USA 62br; incamerastock 33br; Russell Kord 11tr; Simon Leigh 46tl, 59tr; Ninette Maumus 11crb, 16cl; Nikreates 75cl; Sean Pavone 90b; James Quine 23tr; Reuters / Sean Gardner 64b; RM USA 74tl; RosaBetancourt 0 people images 63tr; Philip Scalia 34-5; Stockimo / Penny Hillcrest 65br; Travel Pictures / Pictures Colour Library 4cla; Joe Vogan 7r; WWPics / Matthew D. White 34cl; Jim West 102cl; Paul Wood 12-3; Jennifer Wright 36-7; ZUMAPRESS / Dan Anderson 35tr.

Arnaud's: 58cb, 94ca.

Audubon Nature Institute: 7tc, 21tl, 49br; 72cl, 73t, 81l; Audubon Zoo 18cla, 18-9, 19bc, / Digital Roux Photography LLC 19tl, Digital Roux Photography / Susan Poag 20bl, Digital Roux Photography LLC / Rusty Costanza 20-1; Jeff Strout 10clb, 10crb, 18br, 20cla, 21bl, 48bl.

August: Randy Schmidt 85cb.

BB's Stage Door Canteen: 50cla.

Bridgeman Images: The Historic New Orleans Collection / Acquisition from the Clarisse Claiborne Grima Fund 40tl, Barbara Singer 40cb.

Café Degas: 107b.

Cafe Lafittes: 55cra.

Café NOMA by Ralph Brennan: 13tl.

Cole Pratt Gallery: J. Stephen Young 76tl.

Commander's Palace: 58t.

Courtesy of Arthur Roger Gallery: *Hell Hell Hell Heaven Heaven Heaven: Encountering Sister Gertrude Morgan & Revelation* Lesley Dill October 2010 Exhibition 83bl.

Delmonico: 57ca.

Dreamstime.com: Amadeustx 74b; Bhofack2 56tr, 57tr; Tony Bosse 79br; F11photo 33tr, 65tr; Fotoluminate 29cr; Giovanni Gagliardi 6cla; Jorg Hackemann 3tr, 22bl, 28-9, 108-9; Imagecom 4t; Olivier Le Queinec 4cra; Legacy1995 4b; Maomaotou 4r; Muesfoto 26bc; Sean Pavone 2tl, 3tl, 8-9, 24-5, 26-7, 32-3, 68t, 70-1; Ppy2010ha 56cb; Anthony Aneese Totah Jr 98clb; Lawrence Weslowski Jr 10b, 22-3, 32cl; Colin Young 23cr.

Emeril's: J. Stephen Young 77cr.

The French Market: Chad Boutte 63cl.

LeMieux Galleries: *Contact Tracing* (2015), Aron Belka 80 x 80 inches, oil on canvas / Aron Belka 83cra.

Getty Images: AFP / Robyn Beck 35bc; Bennett Raglin 67cb; FilmMagic / Eric Isaacs 28bl; Erika Goldring 51tr, 53tr, 53cl, 64tc; Tim Graham 31b, 106tr; Liaison / Bryce Lankard 41b; Kylie McLaughlin 97tr; Redferns / Leon Morris 52bl; UIG / Education Images 36bl, 62tl; Warner Brothers 51br; WireImage / Josh Brasted 94b.

Halloween New Orleans: 67tr.

Historic New Orleans Collection: 43r, 90ca.

Houmas House Plantation: Judi Bottoni 69cl.

Howlin' Wolf: 52t.

iStockphoto.com: KarenMassier 1; Gregory Kurpiel 86-7.

Louisiana Children's Museum: 43tl, 49t.

Louisiana State Museum: Mark J. Sindler 26cla.

Mardi Gras World: Jonathan Traviesa 45tr.

Marigny Opera House: Pompo Bresciani 99bl.

Maskarade: Lisa Negrotto 93c.

Mercedes-Benz Superdome: 44br, 80t.

Mother's Restaurant: 61br.

Napoleon House: Chris Granger 95cr.

Courtesy of The National WWII Museum: 42b.

courtesy of the New Orleans Museum of Art Photos by Roman Alokhin and Judy Cooper: 12clb; *Portrait of Mrs. Asher B. Wertheimer*, 1898,

John Singer Sargent, Oil on canvas, purchase in memory of William H. Henderson, 78.3 10ca; *Madonna and Child with Saints*, circa 1340, Benvenuto di Giovanni (follower of), Tempera on wood, The Samuel H. Kress Collection, 61.60 14t; *Kwakiutl, Dance Apron*, circa early 20th century, Unidentified, fabrics, glass beads, brass bells, Gift of an Anonymous Donor, 94.214 14cb; *Portrait of Marie Antoinette, Queen of France*, circa 1788, Elisabeth Louise Vigée Le Brun, Oil on canvas, Museum purchase, Women's Volunteer Committee and Carrie Heiderich Fund, 85.90 15bl; *Unique Forms of Continuity in Space*. 1913 (cast 1931) Umberto Boccioni 103bc; *LOVE, Red Blue*, 1966-1997, Robert Indiana, Aluminum with acrylic polyurethane enamel, 72 x 72 x 36 in.; 182.88 x 182.88 x 91.44 cm, Museum purchase, Sydney and Walda Besthoff Foundation, 2004.119 photo Richard Sexton © Morgan Art Foundation Ltd. / Artists Rights Society (ARS), New York, DACS, London 2017 13br.

New Orleans City Park Archives: 4l, 17tc, 48cr, 103t, 105cl.

New Orleans Wine & Food Experience: Chris Granger 66t.

courtesy Ogden Museum of Southern Art: *Me, Knife, Diamond and Flower* by James Surls, photo Carroll Grevemberg 80clb.

The Outlet Collection at Riverwalk: 84b.

Oxalis: Jian Bastille 101clb.

OZ: 54clb.

Palace Café: Sara Essex Bradley 85cla.

Photoshot: LOOK 69b.

Robert Harding Picture Library: Tim Graham 79t.

The Rodrigue Studio: George Rodrigue 29b.

Satchmo Summer Fest: Zack Smith Photography 66br.

Shaya: 59br.

SuperStock: Seth Resnick 89t.

The Saenger Theatre: 50b.

Trashy Diva: Brittney Werner 62c.

Villa Vici: 76bc.

Cover

Front and spine: **AWL Images:** Danita Delimont
Back: **Dreamstime.com:** Colin Young

Pull Out Map Cover

AWL Images: Danita Delimont

All other images © Dorling Kindersley

For further information see: www.dkimages.com

Penguin
Random
House

Printed and bound in China

First published in Great Britain in 2010
by Dorling Kindersley Limited
80 Strand, London WC2R 0RL

Copyright 2010, 2017 © Dorling
Kindersley Limited

A Penguin Random House Company

17 18 19 20 10 9 8 7 6 5 4 3 2 1

Reprinted with revisions 2012, 2014, 2017

A CIP catalogue record is available from the British Library.

ISBN 978 0 2412 7871 0

MIX
Paper from
responsible sources
FSC™ C018179

SPECIAL EDITIONS OF DK TRAVEL GUIDES

DK Travel Guides can be purchased in bulk quantities at discounted prices for use in promotions or as premiums. We are also able to offer special editions and personalized jackets, corporate imprints, and excerpts from all of our books, tailored specifically to meet your own needs.

To find out more, please contact:

in the US
specialsales@dk.com

in the UK
travelguides@uk.dk.com

in Canada
specialmarkets@dk.com

in Australia
**penguincorporatesales@
penguinrandomhouse.com.au**

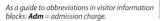
As a guide to abbreviations in visitor information blocks: **Adm** *= admission charge.*

Street Index